Teenagers
Who Tell It All

Teenagers Who Tell It All

Successful Teenagers and Juvenile
Delinquent Teenagers Talk It Out with
Their Mouths and Not with Their Hands

True stories why some teenagers stayed on the right path and
others who failed by the waste side and why they were willing
to help other teenagers stay focused.

A Book for Teenagers and Parents

Angel Flew

Library of Congress Control Number:		2006910378
ISBN:	Hardcover	978-1-4257-4529-5
	Softcover	978-1-4257-4528-8

To order additional copies of this book, contact:
Xlibris Corporation
1-888-795-4274
www.Xlibris.com
Orders@Xlibris.com
36607

To my lovely mother, Mary, whom I respect and love dearly, I truly believe a relationship between a mother and daughter is sent from heaven above. Mother, you are truly a blessing.

To my deceased father, Lee Roy, I could not ask for a better provider because you were differently the number one provider of all times; thank you and may you rest in peace.

LaTia, my beautiful and talented daughter, I'm truly blessed to have you as my daughter; thank you for being understanding and patient. I truly love you.

My siblings Lee, Wanda, Major, and Jackie, I love you all; thank you for being my rock.

To my family, thank you for all your love and support.

I dedicate this book to my nephew Van

I believed in you yesterday, I believe in you today, and I will believe in you tomorrow. I guess in my mind I put you on a pedal stool, thought the world of you, told everyone how intelligent you were and how you were going to enroll in college to make something of your life, something you always talked about ever since you were a kid. I know God spared your life and gave you a second chance, a chance to make you realize how smart, intelligent, talented, brilliant, and bright you really are. Always remember, things happen for a reason; and for whatever the reason maybe, learn from it. I believe we are entitled to one mistake, something we all are guilty of; so in other words, you are, or should I say, we are no different from you. That is why I believe in you yesterday; and I will continue to believe in you tomorrow as well as today because you are brilliant, smart, intelligent, talented, and bright. Van, you are somebody. Not once did I forget about you, not once did a day go by and I didn't think about you. My dear nephew, this was a time in your life you had to walk the road alone, a time to really think things through; sometimes in our lives we have to go through something in order to become somebody. Maybe to you it felt like the world had come to a complete *stop,* when in reality the world was passing you by. Do you remember all the yesterdays that passed your way? Do you remember the season changing from winter to spring, summer, and fall? Do you remember morning changing into night that was yesterday passing you by? But that's okay because you have a second chance, a chance to turn your life around and become the man you were destined to be. Van, I love you, and I truly believe in you, and remember tomorrow is another day. With each passing day, you are getting closer to ending this chapter of this book. Just keep dreaming and keep hope alive.

TEENAGERS WHO TELL IT ALL

True stories why some teenagers made it and others who failed by the waste side.

Some teenagers in this book you will read about say don't give into peer pressure and have respect for yourself, and other teenagers say they had to learn the hard way.

My reason for writing this book is to tell teenagers to never allow anyone or anything stop them from succeeding, such as peer pressure, negative peers, drugs, and their surroundings. Sometimes we think less of our children, and sometimes we put our children on a high pedal stool, but temptation can ruin your child for life. Sometimes as parents, our children do not always listen to us because they feel we do not know anything because we are the parents, which is why I decided to let their peers inform them before it's too late.

The names in this book have been changed to protect their privacy.

Everybody Is Always Talking

Hey! Everybody is talking about you; they say you think you're all that because you wear designer clothes. They say you think you're all that because you got money and you got class. They say you think you're all that because your parents got your back. They say you think you're all that because you drive an expensive car. They say you think you're all that because you live in a fancy house with butlers and maids. They say you think you're all that because you talk proper and not slang. They say you think you're all that because you go to a private school. They say you think you're all that because you always get your way. They say you think you're all that because you travel around the world. They say you think you're all that because you wear diamonds and pearls. They say you think you're all that because your grades are As and Bs and nothing in between.

Well! Let me tell you something everybody say; you don't want nothing, never have and never will. They say you're a follower and not a leader. They say you're nothing because your clothes are old and used. They say you're nothing because you do drugs, and you are only thirteen. They say you're nothing because you walk to school, can't afford a car. They say you're nothing because your parents are unemployed and on drugs. They say you're nothing because you stay in trouble with the law. They say you're nothing because you always use bad judgment, you think wrong is right and right is wrong. They say you're nothing because you dropped out of school, and you will never go to college. If people said the world is coming to an end *tomorrow*, would you believe them? If people said you are going to be rich *tomorrow*, would you believe them? If people said you are going to find gold *tomorrow*, would you believe them? If people said you are going to strike oil *tomorrow*, would you believe them? The bottom line is who cares what people say? They probably don't know you anyway, and if they do, why would you let them upset you? Why would you get mad at words people say? Like they say, sticks and stones may break my bones, but words will never hurt you. If you truly believe that, then who cares if they talk behind your back? *So what* if they talk about your mother, father, sister, or brother? Remember they're only words, and words can never hurt you.

Poem by Angel Flew

Twenty-three years ago, when I was in high school, I remember my girlfriend and I would hang out and have fun; although we were not involved in anything illegal, we had fun, just plain old fun. I remember a new girl came to our school when we were sophomores; because she was new and had no friends, my girlfriend and I became her friends. She was pretty, tall, and slim with long jet-black hair and quiet; even after knowing her for a while, she was still this quiet, laid-back person. She was always in school; she always did her work. I remember we all said we wanted to be professional people; if I recall correctly, she wanted to be a model. A year later, she got pregnant; I never thought in a million years that this quiet person would let this happen to her. After she had the baby, my girlfriend and I went to visit her. Her mother opened the door; and there she was, holding her baby boy. It felt strange because we were young, and she was now a mother; she said she was not going back to school because she didn't have a babysitter, and sure enough she never came back to school. Months later, my girlfriend and I went to visit her; she was acting very strange and weird. She didn't talk much; she was looking at us strange. She was not acting like herself; after we left, we never saw her again. Years later, I heard she was on drugs. Some people said someone put something in her drink at a party, and some said she was on crack. Whatever the case may be, I thought I would never see her again. Until recently, twenty-four years later, I was driving and I saw her standing in front of a store; although I was not sure it was her, because it had been twenty-four years since seeing her. I got out of my car; and as I was approaching her, she called my name. She was filthy, her hair was short dirty and matted; her clothes looked like they had never been washed, her teeth were missing, and the few she had were decayed; her gym shoes were filthy with holes in them. She was walking with a limp; her eyes were yellow, and her body odor smelled like urine. As she was talking to me, she was foaming from the mouth. I could barely understand her speech; tears began to roll down my face. All I could remember was this quiet, pretty, nice girl was now an addict and a bum. She was forty, but she looked like she was every bit of ninety years old. She repeated herself at least three times, very sluggish saying "You remember me, you remember me, you remember me, we went to the same high school." I told her I did remember her, and I asked her what happened and how she got caught up. She said she didn't know what happened to her. Believe me, she didn't know much of anything; although I must admit I was totally surprised that she remembered me.

She asked me for fifty cents; but for some reason, I couldn't give it to her because I knew she was going to use it to get high. Believe me, I wanted to give her more than fifty cents; but for some reason, I couldn't contribute to her addiction. She began telling me her parents passed away, and her son was now twenty-four years old; she also stated her son beat her and took her money, and he threw her out the house. I began to cry even more after she told me that. How could a child mistreat his parent regardless of her situation? She was still his mother. She said she had been on drugs for twenty-four years, and she tried to stop, but she couldn't. Of course, my mind went back to the day when my girlfriend and I went to visit her when she was acting strange, not knowing she was probably high the day we went to visit her. She then asked me for a ride to her brother's house, but I couldn't do it; she was not the same person I knew twenty-four years ago. I did not know the state of mind she was in. After I drove away, I began praying to God, thanking him for keeping me strong. I also asked God to protect and save her. I don't care how you grew up, remember drugs are everywhere in the urban city and the suburban community. Sometimes you don't have to look for trouble, but somehow trouble will always find you. You as an individual can beat the odds, by staying focused and surrounding yourself with positive peers, and remember life is beautiful. Life is as beautiful as *you* make it. Don't let anyone or anything stop you from *your dreams, your successes,* and *your future. You* deserve all of what life has to offer.

Teddy
Age: 16

Tell what it was like growing up: I was the only child. My parents divorced when I was young. I lived at home with my mother. I went to private schools my entire life. I was a straight-A student. My parents did not get along. If they were together for five minutes, they would eventually get into a bad argument, calling each other names; and before you knew it, one of them would leave. They both spoke bad about each other to me; it was rough listening to them down-rate each other as if they hated one another. I often wondered if I was a mistake. I couldn't imagine them ever being affectionate toward one another because they actually hated one another. Being the only child was tough because I had no one to talk to; no one was going through this but me, myself, and I. I always wanted a brother or sister.

Reason why you are in jail: One day, my friends and I skipped school; it was three guys and four girls. The one girl brought alcohol; we all got drunk. No one knew she was going to buy alcohol. She wanted to have sex with my friends and me. I must admit I was scared. We had sex and oral sex; basically, she controlled everything. This was my first time having sex. My biggest fear was what if she gets pregnant; we had no protection. Her friends left the party; they did not get involved. The next day, some of the guys went to school bragging about what happened. Of course, when the girls at the school found out, they began calling her names.

She got upset and left school. She had to defend herself, so she told her parents she was raped. The next thing I knew, the police came to my house to arrest me. I couldn't believe what was happening, me arrested for something we all agreed on.

She wanted sex more than I did. I sat in jail for five days; every thought crossed my mind, how could I be so stupid to let this happen. This was something my mother and I discussed all the time. You read about it in the paper, you see it on television. How could I let this happen? You never think in a million years this could happen to you, especially if both the girl and guy agreed on having sex together. I just knew my life had ended; my plans of graduating from high school going to college were gone overnight in a twinkle of an eye. As I entered the courtroom, I actually thought I was going to pass out. It wasn't a dream; this was reality. Everyone stared at me like I was some rapist; my mother and father for the first time held hands as they both cried. They knew I was innocent. My family and friends wrote letters to the judge, even my pastor, telling the judge the kind of person I was; but it didn't matter. I have never been in any kind of trouble with the law; on my spare time, I was tutoring people with Math, English, and Reading. The judge read the letters that were mailed to her; she announced it in the courtroom. She also stated that she believed I was everything everyone said. I was this nice young man who got caught up for being at the wrong place at the wrong time. The girl and her parents looked and smiled as if they knew I was going away for a long time. The one thing I couldn't understand was this was not the first time this chick did this; it happened three other times to some other guys.

When she went before the judge, she lied about everything, from agreeing to have sex to the outfit she was wearing. I sat there with my mouth opened. I could not believe all the lies this girl was saying, as if she was this innocent person. If only they knew the truth and nothing but the truth, so help me they would be shocked, this girl was a *ho* with a double *h*. A girl who has respect for her body and morals would never stoop so low.

What is it like in jail? At first, I cried every day, morning, noon, and night. I would pray to God to give me strength because he knew I was innocent. I do not wish this on my worse enemy; my freedom is gone. No more hanging out with my friends; no more being with my family for family gathering, especially the holidays; no more talking on the phone; no more eating hot meals; no more sleeping in on weekends, lying back watching television; no more going shopping, buying clothes; no more going outside just to breathe the fresh air. No more freedom; my freedom is gone. Every day I get up at six in the morning because they wake you, and you have to get up or else. I go to bed when they tell me even if I'm not tired; usually the lights are off at nine at night. I lay in my cell and pray to God to help me get through this; it's tough. Sometimes I don't know how I make it; but somehow, in some miraculous way, my Heavenly Father guides me and gives me strength.

What would you tell others to help them? I realize I don't know you. I know nothing about your life, but there is one thing I do know for a fact, and that is if you don't be careful and make wise decisions, this can and will happen to you.

Our parents protect us in many ways. No, they don't hold our hand and put us on their laps, but they talk to us. Sometimes they repeat saying the same thing only to protect us from making mistakes. No, we don't always listen because we don't wanna hear it, because we are going to do what we want even if we sneak. I know we're not perfect, and we all make mistakes, but listening to someone who wants what is best for us, like our parents, relatives, and even an honest, true friend, can help us before we make the wrong decisions.

Peer pressure: I guess everyone looks at peer pressure differently. I never felt pressured or intimidated by anyone. I consider myself a mature young man; my problem was my attitude. I really can't explain why, but I was mainly angry at my parents, I guess for always putting me in the middle of their problems. Although they didn't know it, because I showed no anger directly in front of them because of the respect I had for my parents, but I was angry. When I turned fourteen, I saw myself changing my attitude, I got worse. If it wasn't for my mother staying on my butt about my grades and homework, I probably would have given up; but I knew one thing, my mother didn't play when it came to my grades. Because of her determination I continued to keep a grade point average of 3.5. The one thing I realize the most is, it does matter if your grade point average is 4.0 or 2.0; if you want something out of life, nothing and nobody will be able to stop you.

To parents: Keep praying for your child. Don't give up on them and continue to help them. Parents, we need you because you are the link to our future and the solution to our problems. Everything my mother told me came to pass, but I didn't listen, but through it all, I will never forget how my mother tried to protect me, and because of that, I can truly say I love her for everything she did for me.

Theresa
Age: 17

What was it like growing up? My mother was a b——. She put everything before me, especially her menfolk. My mother was dating this guy whom she really knew nothing about before he moved in with us. If I'm not mistaken, she knew him only three weeks before he moved in with us. Seven months later, he raped me; and later, I founded out he raped my sister as well. My mother did not believe us; she called my sister and me names and told us we better not tell anyone that lie or she would leave us and move away with Earl. My sister and I, of course, were terrified. I have no respect for my mother or any parent that would defend some low-down jerk over their children.

Reason why you are in juvenile: I was angry and mad. I didn't care about anything. I stayed in and out of trouble.

What is it like in juvenile? At first, I didn't care about being locked up. I didn't care about anything until I came here; now I can say I care about things. Now I'm not a bad person. I realize now those things that happened to me were not my fault. Although I don't like being locked up, I can truly say this place saved my life.

What would you tell others to help them? Enjoy being young. Please don't rush it, because everything is not going to go your way. But remember, everything happens for a reason; and remember one thing, God loves you even if the world is against you.

Peer pressure: You know when people do wrong, they refuse to do wrong by themselves. But when people are doing good, they want the gold for themselves; they aim for the gold.

To parents: Just like it's hard to find good friends, it's twice as hard to be good parents.

Kevin
Age: 17

What was it like growing up? I grew up in and out of foster homes. My mother was on drugs; my father was in prison. I only met him twice; each time was in prison. My mother was a very confused person; she started molesting me when I was a kid. I thought it was normal. I actually thought this was something all kids did for their parent. I remember when I was eight years old, I went to school and told my teacher; she couldn't believe what I was saying. The look on her face I would never forget. She took me to the principal's office; the next thing I knew, the authority and the social workers were at my school. I still didn't realize anything was wrong.

Reason why you are in juvenile: This girl and I got together and had sex at her parent's house when they were at work. This particular day, her father came home early, he caught us having sex; she got scared and told her father I broke in and raped her. Her father was a huge guy; he held me until the police came. I couldn't believe she told a lie like that. I was scared because I knew I was in trouble. I begged her to please tell the truth, but she never changed her story. I truly believe her father and the police knew she was lying.

What is it like in juvenile? I hate this place because I know I'm innocent, but there is nothing I can do.

What would you tell others to help them? Think before you act, because you never know what the outcome is going to be; and remember, whatever you do, don't lie on someone just because you can. Do the right thing and be honest because one day it will come back and haunt you.

Peer pressure: Peer pressure is not the problem; it's the person trying to make peer pressure the problem.

To parents: Stop being lazy; take care of your child. Your child is your responsibility, not your mother, father, sister, or brother. Do your job and take care of your child.

Baba
Age: 17

What was it like growing up? My mom stayed in and out of prison my whole life. *That's messed up*; she is no mother to me. I don't even call her mom. I call her by her first name, Cheryl, and believe me she gotten a lot of names and social security number. I wish like hell; I had another mother, because a mother she's not.

Reason why you are in juvenile: I started hanging out with the wrong people, and we did things I'm not too proud to talk about.

What is it like in juvenile? All I can say is don't come here. There is nothing nice or pretty about this place.

What would you tell others to help them? You don't need friends in order to feel you belong, but just in case make sure you pick your friends like you pick your clothes, with class. I feel like I am making the same mistakes Cheryl made, and I refuse to be like her. I knew the people I was hanging around with were trouble;

but sometimes you don't think clearly. You feel like people don't understand you, and you don't care about anything; believe me, I know how you feel. If I could do things over, I will definitely do things different; believe me, you don't want to be locked up. It is not worth losing your freedom once you get locked up; you never know how long you will be lock up.

To parents: I can't judge all parents the same because I know of some damn good parents; and to those parents who love and take good care of their kids, I have nothing but respect for you and to my so-called mother. I rest my case.

Cage
Age: 17

Tell what it was like growing up: Both of my parents devoted all their time and energy into their jobs. They both had excellent jobs; whatever I wanted I got, it didn't matter how much it cost. I got fairly good grades. I was involved with sports when I turned fourteen. I guess you can say I changed. I don't know why, but I did; everyone said it was peer pressure, but I'm not sure.

Reason why you are in juvenile: I started using drugs; and from there, I got in trouble with the law.

What is it like in juvenile? This place is not for me. I understand why I'm here. I just don't know how long I'm going to be here.

What would you tell others to help them? Stay in school, just stay active and enjoy your teenage years; it only lasts a short time. Until this day, I cannot believe I allowed myself to get caught up; it's not because I didn't know better. My friends whom I was hanging around with were doing it, so I did it just to fit in. We always think it can't happen to us; believe me, if you hang around with people who are doing wrong, eventually you will find yourself doing the exact thing. You might not think so; but believe me, you will, like they say birds of the feathers flock together. Believe me, once you try drugs, more than likely you will continue; and when that happens, you are then an addict. Please don't get caught up with the wrong crowd; it's that simple.

Peer pressure: Peer pressure is all around us; you can't escape it. The only thing I can say is don't give in to it. If you stay active with different activities, you will be all right.

To parents: Sometimes being a teenager is difficult because of peer pressure and all the negative things we often see, but I also know if you teach your child what is right, they will find themselves remembering all the good things you taught and showed them.

Bridgett
Age: 17

Tell what it was like growing up: My mother and I along with my brother and sisters were damn near homeless; we got evicted everywhere we moved. My mother would never pay her bills; my sister and brother moved with their dad. My dad was sorry. When I was sixteen, I ran away from home. Each time we were evicted, we would move with a relative or friends; it was hard. I always felt like we were in the way. My mother didn't care; she had no shame. My father is no better; he had children everywhere as if it was something to be proud of. I have no respect for him at all. How could you father children and not take care of them? He's a bum and a loser

Reason why you are in juvenile; I kept running away from home.

What is it like in juvenile? This place is for teenagers that are really out of control. I don't feel like I'm out of control.

Pregnancy: There are so many girls here who have kids, and their kids are in foster care; more than likely, they will remain in foster care until someone adopts them. It's really sad; the one thing I would say is don't get pregnant first, experience all of what life has to offer you.

Peer pressure: I always wonder, do kids whose parents have money deal with peer pressure differently, or is it something teenagers experience regardless?

To parents: Be a friend, mother, and father to your child.

Alan
Age: 17

What was it like growing up? My mother was on drugs, I lived with my grandmother and aunt. I can recall the time when I went on a trip with my sixth grade class. My mother saw me and came over to me. Of course, my friends and teacher were looking.

I was embarrassed and was ashamed; my mother asked me for $2.00. Everyone knew that was my mother because they saw her before. I never wanted to go back to that school because I thought everyone was going to make fun of me and my mother. When I went to school the next day, some kids made fun of my mother, but most of them were understanding; they acted as if nothing happened.

Reason why you are in juvenile: I joined the gang; and from there, I was out of control, because I was angry with my mother and father for not being in my life. So instead, I turned to crime for the answer.

What is it like in juvenile? You have no life; it's terrible. I miss going outside especially on hot summer days. I hear traffic constantly; people having a good time, but I'm locked up, it hurts.

What would you tell others to help them? Do the right thing; don't get caught up with negative people. Use your mind and think. I know you don't know me, and you are probably saying I don't know what I'm talking about, and it's your life. You are right; I don't know you; and believe me, I don't want anything to happen to you because it's not worth it. I hope, one day, to continue helping others so they won't end up in a place like this or perhaps worse.

Peer pressure: Like I said, stay in control and don't let anyone control you.

To parents: Don't be like my mother; love your child unconditionally. We want our parents to support us, love us, and pamper us. Believe me, I pray for peace and happiness every day because God has given me another chance to turn my life around; and believe me, I have.

Mark
Age: 17

What was it like growing up? I was raised by both my mom and dad. My father would get mad about any little thing. He would beat my brother, sister, and me. Because I was the oldest, I got beat more than the others; I remember my father beat me so bad I threw up. My mother said or did nothing; she would cry, but she never defended us.

Reason why you are in juvenile: I joined a gang. I wanted to do my father in for all the pain he caused my siblings and me. I hate that mother-fucker he's a coward.

What is it like in juvenile? It feels like I'm still getting beat by father mentally and physically.

What would you tell others to help them? Hopefully, you don't have a jackass for a father if you do, I understand how you feel the anger and the frustration can be unbearable but regardless don't stoop so low and lose respect for yourself don't become like them, be better just remember what goes around comes around.

Pregnancy: I know I don't want any babies. I can't see myself getting some girl pregnant. So fellows, be careful. Don't get caught up and protect yourself—or else.

To parents: Man, my parents left me hanging; not one of them came to visit or call me. The one thing my parents taught me was not to be like them. Once I leave this place, I promise I will never look back

Jazzy
Age: 17

What was it like growing up? Growing up for me was tough; my mother was always jealous of me. She would always put me down; she was like a friend but not a best friend. She dated only young men when I was fifteen; her so-called boyfriend was twenty-one, and my mother is forty-three. One day, he asked me for sex. He said I was closer to his age than my mother; he was fine, I must admit. So one day, I came home early from school because we had plans to be together. He didn't work; my mother took care of him. She would buy him clothes, food, cigarettes, and liquor just to keep him. She would buy him things all the time, but she would never buy me anything. When I told her about it, she said I was not her daughter; and for me to get my own man, then she called me a *hoe*.

Reason why you are in juvenile: I started dating this guy. My mother's boyfriend found out of course; he got jealous, I mean really jealous. He told me to stop talking to him, but I didn't because I liked him.

Well, to make a long story short, he lied and told my mother I asked him to go to bed with me, and my mother believed him over me. She told me to get out her house, then she called me every name in the book. I had no place to go. Before I knew, it she punched me in the face. I was so angry I hit her back. We began rolling on the floor. She pulled my hair, I pushed hers. She was calling me names,

I was calling her names. Her boyfriend called the police; my mother press charges. They both said I started the whole thing, and I was out of control.

What is it like in juvenile? I don't like it; they fight all the time, and they will pick a fight with you for no reason. So you better know how to defend yourself, or you will be sorry.

What would you tell others to help them? Just because things may be rough at home, keep your head up and keep praying; because one day, things will get better for you.

Pregnancy: To all the teenagers out there who think they are ready for a child, please think about it; don't get caught up. My mother had my brother when she was fourteen. She struggled; my uncle told me, my brother's father and my mother were so in love. After my mother had my brother, my brother's father moved to another state and started college. After getting his degree, he married a lady he met in college, and they both are doing well. It was so hard for my mother to raise my brother on her own, financially; she gave him up for adoption. I often wonder what he look like; many times, I wish I had a sibling, being the only child is boring sometimes. I hope my brother is happy. I'm sure they probably love him better than my mother loved him.

Peer pressure: You know, I have been through so much with my mother if peer pressure slapped me in the face, I wouldn't know the difference.

Kim
Age: 17

What was it like growing up? I was raised by my father; my mother was on drugs, and my father was an alcoholic. I remember when I was in school I received the honor award for receiving straight As on my report card. The ceremony started at 6:00 p.m. When I got home from school, my father was so drunk; he couldn't hold his head up. I went to the ceremony by myself; my classmates and their parents were there, even their relatives. Whenever someone's name was called, they asked for the family member of each child to stand. Because I received the highest award, they had more to say about me; when they asked my family members to stand, no one stood. One of my teachers looked around, like everyone else to see who would stand; so my teacher stood for me and they applauded my teacher. I felt so alone; but on the other hand, I felt proud to have a teacher like her. I can truly say she eased the pain I was feeling for that moment.

Reason why you can in juvenile: I started using drugs at the age of fifteen. I guess you can say I was addicted; I couldn't stop. Drugs eased the pain I was feeling; I felt like I didn't belong. I had low self-esteem; my life was worthless. I got caught shop lifting so I could buy drugs to support my habit.

What is it like in juvenile? I guess the harder thing about being here is that I'm not a bad person. I'm someone who needs help.

What would you tell others? If you are at a down point in your life and you feel like you can't go on, believe me, it will get better; you may not think so, but I promise you it will. Remember, you are never by yourself; this is a big world. I'm sure everyone in has hit rock bottom; there are some people who have lost everything they own. There are people who are going through worse things than you are; if you don't believe me, just look around you. If you have faith, believe me, you will come out on top. I thought no one loved me because my mother was on drugs; I can count the times I ever saw her. My father is an alcoholic. I have no family; but I know one thing, at least I know it now. I don't need anyone to love me because I love myself, and that's enough love for me. Don't expect for everyone to love you or accept you; as a matter of fact, it's best if they don't. Be yourself, but be the best you can be, and your life will only get better.

Peer pressure: Don't let anyone tell you the negative things about peer pressure. Peer pressure is also something positive; so remember, it's only what you make it to be. If you decide to do something you know you shouldn't do, don't blame it on peer pressure because you are in control of yourself.

Pregnancy: I know I don't know you, but don't let anyone talk you into having a baby; because no matter what, the girl, more than likely, will be raising the child. There are a lot of girls in here with babies and none is with the father (*not one*).

To parents: Take time out with your child, talk to them, and listen to them without fussing. Remember, we learn from you. Introduce them to positive things; be honest and talk to them about sex and about life. Remember, being a good parent is not based on being a mother or father; it's based on being a role model, setting examples, and being a leader.

Kenny
Age: 17

What was it like growing up? My mother and father both sold drugs from our home; my brother, sister, and I knew what they were doing because the drugs were kept in the closet inside a chest with magazines and books on top of it. Different people would come to the house every day; I mean every day, in the morning until late at night. It was hard to sleep with all the noise and people laughing and talking loud at one and two in the morning. My sister and brother dropped out of school first, then I dropped out. My parents didn't mind; as a matter of fact, my brother and sister both started selling drugs, and of course, I followed.

Reason why you are in juvenile: I got caught selling drugs.

What is it like in juvenile? I knew one day I was going to get caught. I'm not happy about it because I don't like it here. I feel like I'm trapped in this box, and there is no way out. I've been here for two years, and I'm tired. Juvenile detention is not a place where you go and leave when you are tired; you actually stay until the judge release you. Sometimes it can take forever.

What can you tell others to help them? Don't let anyone influence you to do what is wrong. I don't care who it is, your mother, father, sister, or brother; believe me, it's not worth it. If I could do things over, I promise you I wouldn't do anything that would cause me to lose my freedom.

Peer pressure: I feel like my own parents pressured me to sell drugs; never again. Until this day, I have not heard or talked to my parents.

To parents: Although my parents are living, I feel like they are actually dead; this has taught me that sometimes your parents can be your worse enemy.

Alisa
Age: 17

What was it like growing up? My mother partied every day; she would dress with tight blue jeans with holes up to her butt. Sometimes she was damn near nude with every parts of her body hanging out. She had a girlfriend whom she would be with all the time. They both dated men that were married; my mother would always say if they were married, they can't tell me who to date and who to sleep with. She would tell me that all the time. Even though I knew it was wrong, I wanted to try it because my mother made it seem as if it was okay; she always had money because these men would give money to her. My mom had five different men she was dating, and she had others that she would see from time to time.

Reason why you are in juvenile: I started stripping at a nightclub and prostituting.

What is it like in juvenile? Everyone always tell you what you can or cannot do, and you get in trouble for the least little thing. For instance, if I make my bed up wrong, I get in trouble; if I don't eat my food, they write me up. If I'm not out of bed at a certain time, I get in trouble; you would not believe how much trouble you could get in.

What would you tell others to help them? I used to watch kids on television who were being out of control and the parents didn't know what to do. I understand how the kids felt because I was going through the same thing; but I am here to tell you it's not worth it, because once you get in trouble, it is *so, so, so, so* hard to get out of it. I have been locked up for ten freaking months, and I don't know when I'm going home. My whole life is in the judge's hand; and if for any reason he feel I'm not ready to go home, then I'm not going to. The judge knows exactly what you are doing at all times because he receives your daily reports. Sometimes if the kids don't like you or if they find out you are leaving soon, they will make it hard for you. Some would start a fight with you and that will cause the judge to keep you locked up longer; so believe me when I tell you this, you don't have friends when you are in a place like this. I can bet you one thing; you will never find one person who will tell you they like being locked up. The one thing I can say is do not get into trouble, and you won't get locked up.

Edward
Age: 18

What was it like growing up? It was okay, nothing special; both of my parents worked. My mom and dad have been married for twenty-three years; my two sisters and I are close. I'm their only brother; we took family vacations when we were younger. It was okay to me; it was normal.

Reason why you are in juvenile: When I got to high school, I started hanging out with the wrong crowd, cutting classes, getting high, and having sex, you name it. This one particular day, some friends and I skipped school; we were walking, and the next thing I know the police stopped us. This old man got robbed and was beat up; because it was during school hours, everyone was in school at that time except us. The police assumed it was us; they took us where the incident took place, which was only four blocks away. The old man was so shaking up and said we were the one. I never being so scared in my life because we skipped class; I knew we were in deep trouble. When my parents found out, they thought I didn't do it because I was in school. How could I tell my parents I was not in class. When they found out the truth, the pain and hurt on my parent's face nearly killed me. Both of my parents cried; I couldn't believe I caused all this pain to my parents.

What is it like in juvenile? It's hard especially because I'm innocent. I would never cause pain to anyone especially elderly people. When you are locked up, you lose your freedom. I mean, it's really hard, and it's frightening because I don't know when I'm going home. I've been here for two years.

What would tell others to help them? I hope teenagers that are reading my story really think before they act. Listen, I knew skipping classes was wrong, but what I didn't know was what was going to happen next. If you know you are doing something wrong, please don't do it. If your friend comes to you and asks you to come along, don't be stupid. If they can't understand that, you do not wish to get involved, and if they get upset, who cares. Think before you say yes if you're smart; with some common sense, you better say no. Remember, if you do wrong, wrong will come back on you; and if you do right, right will come back to you as well; it's up to you.

Peer pressure: Think for yourself; don't let others think for you and don't think everybody is your friend. All you need is one friend, and sometimes you don't need one. Your best friend is yourself; I had to learn the hard way, but you don't have to. Don't get caught up in peer pressure; the choice is yours. So don't be stupid or else you will end up where I'm at. So if you think it can't happen to you because you're cool and slick, keep doing what you're doing; I promise you, you will soon be where I'm at in, juvenile or jail.

To parents: First, I would like to tell my parents I'm sorry for making them shame; and everything they did for me, I appreciate them for that. I believe if parents teach their child what is right, they should never feel guilty for their child's action; sometimes they have to fall on their head before they get any sense. I just hope when they do fall, it won't be fatal. I know the day when I leave this place, I going to register for college; this is not a life for me.

Sherri
Age: 17

What was it like growing up? My mother was in and out of jail. Everything she did was illegal; doing what was right was not her nature. My mother would shoplift from department stores in front of my sisters and me. Sometimes she made us take our school bag so she could put things inside our book bag.

Reason why you are in juvenile: I joined a gang, and we did illegal things; looking back at all the wrong I did, I'm not proud of myself.

What is it like in juvenile? It's hard because you can't do anything; you can't talk on the phone when you want, and you can't call whoever you want. There are rules you must follow; everybody is always watching you. It's hard. I don't like it.

What would you tell others to help them? Stay focused. Don't let anyone tell you what to do; make your own decisions. You don't need friends, especially friends that are in gangs, because the bottom line is they are not your friends. Ask anyone who has dealt with gang members. People who join the gang join for all the wrong reasons. Usually, people who join the gang are afraid to be by themselves; they feel like they need these people for protection. At that moment, they may be down with you; but they will never support you. They don't have your back, never did, and never will; some may even turn on you like a pit bull. No matter what problems you are going through with family or peers, it will only last for a while, not a lifetime. Just hang in there and pray for these people because actually they are asking for help.

Peer pressure: If you are dealing with peer pressure, talk to someone like a good friend or someone who will tell you the truth and take their advice even if it hurts. Don't expect for everyone to agree with you; sometimes it's best if they don't, and remember that an honest, true friend only wants what's best for you, even if you don't agree with what they are saying.

To parents: Please be a role model to your child because what they see you do more than likely will reflect them as they grow into adulthood.

Mickey
Age: 17

What was it like growing up? My mother was a single parent of three; she was a hardworking person, she attended college for two years before she stopped, she taught us right from wrong, and she also told us to be careful whom we pick as friends. For the summer, we usually go visit family members from out of state. I can honestly say she did her best to provide for us.

Reason why you are in juvenile: I started hanging out with the wrong crowd, something my mother always told me not to do; but I was hardheaded, not realizing it would catch up with me. The guys I was hanging out with stole a car; although I didn't steal it, because I was with them, the judge said I was also responsible for the crime.

What is it like in juvenile? I don't like it because the guys here are trouble; man, I try my best to stay to myself, but it's hard as hell. They fight almost every day over simple stuff; and if you're not apart of their click, they constantly pick on you, and you have to defend yourself or they will kick your ass. This place suck, I mean really suck.

What would you tell others to help them? If you are hanging around a bad group of people, all I can say is stop flat out because the bottom line is they don't have your back. They talk a good game, but actually, they ain't down with you.

Peer pressure: Ask yourself if you're a leader or a follower; if you feel you can't make your own decisions, learn to be strong and don't let anybody control you and push you around.

To parents: My mother is my role model, my backbone, and my friend; everything she taught me was right. Although I had to learn the hard way, I will never forget all the talks we shared, all the advice she gave me because she loved and wanted only the best for me. At the time, I thought I knew it all; what she said to me didn't matter. Now I look back at the things I did, and I really feel ashamed of myself because I can't take back the things I did; once you do something to someone or commit to a crime, you can never take that back. Although I never committed a crime, I know of people who have; their lives would never be the same. As a matter of fact, it would only get worse.

I know guys who have fifteen years to life in prison, and they can't do anything to change it; once you are sentenced, that's it. Just think, if a person commits to a crime and it took only five minutes to commit to that crime, from that day on, you will be living a different life; a life that is not normal and that is not of God. Actually, you have no purpose and that crime will cause you the rest of your life; your freedom is gone. I would whether be dead before I lose my freedom; actually, a part of you is dead. Parents, keep talking to your children, give them hugs and kisses, tell them how much you love them, and show them the way to be a role model. To all my peers, listen and learn; I know we are not perfect, but we're not stupid. Remember, you don't need friends; if they don't want the best for you or if you know they're jealous, stay away from them, far away because they mean you no good.

Stanley
Age: 17

What was it like growing up? My brother and I were raised by our father; my mother married this guy who wanted no parts of my brother and me. I remember, when I would go visit my mother, her husband would always talk bad to her about my brother and me. I can recall the last time we saw our mother, her husband accused my brother and me of stealing; we were only six and seven. He said we stole his checkbook and $200.00. My mother believed him; she checked our clothes and our suitcase. She said if we didn't tell her the truth, she would call the police, and we would go into a foster home. We told our mother the truth, but she said we were lying; she called our father. Our father came to pick us up, and we never saw our mother again.

Reason why you are in juvenile: These boys had beef with me and were going to jump on me, so I had to protect myself. I took a gun to school, the teacher found out, and the rest is history.

What is it like in juvenile? You don't wanna come here; you can't do anything without getting permission. I see more fights here than any place I've ever being. If you don't get it together here, you will never get it together.

What would you tell others to help them? If someone threatens you, tell someone; don't do anything, you may regret later. It's not that you're scared, you just don't wanna get caught up and have to pay a price for it later; why lose your freedom for someone else foolishness. At one time, I thought violence was the answer; I realized now I had low self-esteem, being rejected by my mother was very painful. I never understood how my mother could hate my brother and me. After soul searching, I realized my mother has a problem within herself. I can now go on with my life knowing I'm not responsible for my mother's behavior. I received my GED I will be entering college when I leave here.

Peer pressure: Distance yourself from people that are trouble, people that talk bad about others, people that think crime is the answer, and people who basically want nothing out of life. You have to realize you are *not* responsible for their behavior. If they don't wish to change, don't waste your time trying to change them.

I hear people talking about peer pressure when it comes to teenagers; listen, you know right from wrong. If you take someone's life, don't blame it on peer pressure because you knew what the hell you were doing. The bottom line is this, if you can't find an honest friend, stay to yourself at least; then you know you are focused. Why get caught up in something that can damage your life forever? Why would *you* let someone change you for the worse; it makes no sense be in control of your own life? Remember, your life, body, and mind belongs to you, so don't let anyone take that away from you. If you don't believe me, look in the mirror. Who do you see looking back at you? Tell yourself every day I'm strong, I'm a leader, and I am somebody, and believe it. I look back at the mistake I made for carrying a gun; although at the time I didn't care, I was trying to protect myself. I ask myself, time and time again, what would have happened if I shot those guys? It's not worth being locked up. I feel worst now than before because my freedom is gone, and I didn't solve anything. Of course, I have time to look back at the mistake I made, and it upsets me because I'm a person who doesn't look for trouble, but that particular day, trouble came looking for me. I truly believe it could have been avoided; there are ways we can handle certain situations. I'm mad at myself for allowing them to push my buttons, and because of that I am paying a price for it.

To parents: I understand, being a parent is not easy, but it's not as hard as some parents make it to be. My father was a single parent; I know for a fact that it doesn't take a village to raise a child. It takes a strong-minded, loving parent to raise a child. Even through I made mistakes, I never forgot the tough love my father showed me; his favorite words were, father to son, man to man, and if I should fall, I will get up and stand straight and tall like a proud man.

Jasmine
Age: 17

What was it like growing up? I lived with both parents; my parents have being married for twenty years. Growing up was okay; although they were married, they were not together as a couple. Ever since I could remember they both slept in separate bedrooms, and they both dated other people. I met my father's girlfriend several times; my mother's boyfriend was always a secret. I often wondered if she really had one. I went to a pretty decent high school; you don't see fights or kids doing drugs on the premise. I was not involved with different activities; I had my baby when I was fifteen.

Reason why you are in juvenile: My baby's father is an older guy; he was a drug dealer. We were together at his friend house. The house got raided for drugs; because I was there when this took place, I was also convicted.

What is it like in juvenile? I miss my baby so much; this place is not for me. I feel like a criminal, a heartless criminal. When we leave the premises for doctor visits or whatever, you have to wear these ugly uniforms, and they handcuff you because it's the law. Whenever you are locked up in a facility, you will be treated as a criminal. It is so embarrassing to wear handcuff to doctor visits; of course, everyone is looking at you as if you are some vicious animal ready to attack. Everyone treats you differently, and there is nothing you can do. I remember this one time, some of the girls had doctor appointments; they started talking loud. It was no big deal; they said nothing wrong. One of the staff members at our facility made all of us stand because we were out of order. We had to stand in a circle in front of all the people in the clinic and repeat these words out loud to each other, which were how to act when you are in public. I was so embarrassed; I actually wanted to crawl under a rock and die. Everyone looked at us as if we were freaks. The thing I would like to say is don't put yourself in a situation where you have to go into juvenile; it's not what you think, and I truly believe it is going to get worse. People are tired of all the crime and destructive behavior, so please get it together, or you will find yourself here. I, being here for one year and three months, have no idea when I will be leaving. I know I should have been out before now; but the bottom line is once you are in the system, you have no control of your life anymore.

Pregnancy: I love my son with all my heart; he is everything to me. I feel as if I cheated him out of a better life. I want so much for my son, but I can't give him much, especially since I'm locked up. Even if I wasn't locked up, I still wouldn't be able to supply all his needs.

If you are thinking about having a baby, please think really hard; be honest to yourself and to the child you are thinking of having. Ask yourself if you can afford a baby on your income, not your mother, father, or the baby's father's income because there are no guarantees that these people will support you. Remember, it's not their responsibility, because you wanted this baby; no matter what, this is your baby and only your baby. Ask yourself if you are mentally ready, and remember every day of her life will be with this baby. Every breath you take will be for this baby; your life will change in a way you can't imagine.

Peer pressure: Just because peer pressure exists, you don't have to be apart of it; if you are dealing with peer pressure or if you are having problems with someone, find someone you can trust. Talk to them; you will be surprised how they can help, especially if they're older. You have to realize, as long as you are living in this world, we will face difficulties; if not today, one day. So don't feel like you are by yourself; there's a whole world out there with people and problems greater than yours. So remember, problems don't last forever.

To parents: As parents, it is so important that you talk and teach your child, right from wrong. When your child was little, they were learning to put their shoes on, and because they didn't know better, they probably placed their shoes on the wrong foot; did you tell them that the right shoe went on the right foot, and the left on the left foot? Or you didn't care; you just like them go outside with their shoes on the wrong foot? Life is no different if you don't teach your child right from wrong at an early age, why would you not think you are not responsible for they actions? Be a parent and take charge; teach your child values and mortals and don't leave it up to us. Remember, you're the parent, not us.

JD
Age: 17

What was it like growing up? I'm the youngest of five. We all had different fathers; my father was in prison. I would visit him sometimes; he is doing time for attempted murder. He said it was self-defense, of course, I will never know. My mother has always been in and out of relationships. If a man don't pay her bills or give her money, she would get involved in another relationship. Ever since I could remember, that's how it's been. It was rough growing up; we barely had clothes to wear to school. Sometimes we didn't go to school because we had nothing to wear. Because my birthday was two months before Christmas, I had to wait until Christmas for my birthday and Christmas prize.

Reason why you are in juvenile: I was caught with drugs and a weapon.

What is it like in juvenile? It really doesn't bother me, but I would rather not be here.

What would you tell others to help them? If you are doing something you should not be doing, eventually you will be caught; it's easy to get in trouble, but it's hard as hell to get out of trouble.

Peer pressure: I'm not down with peer pressure. What the hell is that anyway?

To parents: Have respect for your kids, but most of all, have respect for yourself. Don't bring home every Tom, Dick, and Harry; if you do, at least sneak. Don't involve your kids in your private life. And don't blame us for not having respect for you when you don't have respect for your damn self.

John
Age: 18

What was it like growing? Both my parents were drug addicts; we lived from place to place and with whomever. It was hard and difficult, most of the time; sometimes my cousin would let us stay with her until my father stole from her to buy drugs for him and my mother. Once my cousin found out, she put us out; so we lived on the streets and in alleys under boxes so rats and dogs didn't bite us. We smelled like garbage. Our clothes had holes in them, our hair was dirty, we couldn't brush our teeth, we would urinate in the alley, and everything else. My father's brother eventually took us in. We lived there until my mother got a job at a fast food restaurant; later, we moved into an old run-down flat, bums and crackheads on every corner, but it was a place where we could lay our head. I started doing drugs when I was thirteen, only to kill the pain and hurt; it was hard for me to cope with reality. Being poor is very hard, not knowing if you were going to eat tomorrow and not knowing if you were going to have a place to lay your head, because my parents were on drugs. I knew their priorities were not in the right place.

Reason why you are in juvenile: I started selling drugs at fourteen to support my parents and me.

What is it like in juvenile? At least I have a bed to sleep on; but more than anything, I wish I wasn't here. But I know it's going to be okay; I feel more safe here than at home.

What would you tell others to help them? No matter what you are going through, keep doing the right thing, because it will get better; nothings stays the same. Just hold on because a door will soon open for you. Keep praying, talk to God, tell him your problems, and be honest and he will fix it.

Pregnancy: I'm a young father. I feel like the world has stopped. I'm not ready to take on responsibility of being a father, but it's too late to cry wolf.

To parents: Remember, we didn't ask to be born; take care of your responsibilities. At least, I will. Little John, I love you.

JC
Age: 17

What was it like growing up? My mother and stepfather were very strict; both of my parents are college grads. We lived in the suburb, a highly respected community. I was forced to be involved in different activities; actually. I had no say so, especially when it came to school academic. My brother and sisters were pretty smart. They never had problems with school; but on the other hand, school was not a thing for me because I had a problem keeping up. My parents would always tell me I wasn't trying hard enough, and my brother and sister were going to go further in life because they are determined. I never could understand why they would put me down but reward my siblings. Believe me, it's not because I didn't try, because I always tried my best; but to my parents, it wasn't enough. I always felt different. I never felt important like everyone else; my parents didn't care how it affected me. My sisters and brother would call me stupid and dumb. I knew it was wrong, but what could I do; I definately couldn't go to my parents because they would say nothing.

Reason why you are in juvenile: I started hanging out with the wrong crowd of people; and from there, I started doing drugs.

What is it like in juvenile? Regardless of how I felt at home, I now know what they mean when they say there is no place like home.

What would you tell others to help them? No matter how hard things may seem, believe me, it's really not that bad. Cherish every moment, good or bad, because when it is taken away from you, you then realize it really wasn't that bad. The way my parents and siblings acted toward me, I know they care. Although they went about it the wrong way, it was the only way they knew how. My parents are not affectionate; they don't embrace one another with hugs and kisses, and neither do my brother and sisters. Once, I realized that I was able to deal with my family in a positive way. The name calling and the tough love, regardless, that's my family, the only family I will ever have through thick and thin to death do us part. The one thing we must remember, no matter what, your family will always have your back.

Even though it may not seem that way, or if they tell you, they don't, or even if you all are not speaking, they got your back; because if something was to happen to you, that little thing inside of them called love will show its face. It may be too late for them to tell you they're sorry, but believe me they will say it. You may hear them when they say it, or you may not hear them, but they will say it. Remember, everyone can't forgive, like the next person; it's only because they don't know how. It's not because they don't want to, they just don't know how. It may be easy for one person to forgive but hard for the next. The best thing to do is tell them you're sorry and give them room to inhale it.

Peer pressure: If you have a strong loving family or a parent who is willing to help you, accept the offer because the bottom line is there is nobody like your family. Or if you have a good friend who wants what is best for you, talk to them; sometimes they can and will help. Never tell everybody your problems, only tell people you can honestly trust.

Parents: Please try your best to be the best parent you could be. We know parents are not perfect, but at least, be a role model so your child won't have to look to someone else to be their role model. Sometimes the role model they chose may be the wrong one.

Terri
Age: 16

What was it like growing up? My mother died when I was ten years old; my father raised my sister and me. He was in and out of relationships. I think he tried to find a mother for my sister and me. I never felt love by any of the women my father dated; either they were jealous of the relationship we had with our father, or they were pretending to like us because they were trying to get closer to my father.

Reason why you are in juvenile: I got pregnant when I was fourteen. I thought I was a grown up and no one could tell me anything; my grandmother would tell my father I was disrespectful. She was right; I just didn't care. I started hanging out all night; sometimes I didn't come home for two to three days, depending on what was going on. My father turned me over to the authority; he said I was out of control.

What is it like in juvenile? Of course, I wish I were at home with my family, especially my baby. I realize things happen for a reason; something it takes falling on your face before you wake up. Juvenile is not a place for anyone; what person in their right mind would prefer to be locked up in some place where you can't do anything. Anything you do, you have to ask for permission; you can't even go to the bathroom without asking for permission. Majority of the times, you have to stand in line to go to the restroom. You have no privacy; it sucks. You can't sit down and relax for a bath, only showers. You can't write letters and send them out unless staff read it, and they read every letter people mail you. Your personal items you receive have to be searched by the people who work in the facility; if they say you can't have it, you can't have it. It's that simple.

What would you tell others to help them? Don't get caught up with the wrong people, because more than likely, you will eventually find yourself right here. Believe me, there is room. Don't let people convince you into doing something you know is wrong because you never know who is watching you; it is so important for us to learn to say *no*, especially if you know it's wrong.

Peer pressure: Like I said, learn how to say no; usually the other person will follow you. Remember, no one wants to be by themselves when they are doing wrong. People who make negative decisions are not leaders; only the people who lead others into doing what is right are leaders.

To parents: Dad, I love you; thank you for all you did. I realize now you did your best to raise us. When I now look in the mirror, I see a person who is willing to make a change a person who had to learn the hard way. I'm happy to be given another chance; and when I look in the mirror, I also see you, Dad.

David
Age: 17

What was it like growing up? I lived with my mother and sister; I'm the oldest. My mother was never home to care for my sister and me; I felt like I was the parent. I was two grades behind; I barely went to school. School was not important to me.

I am worried constantly about my mother, not knowing where she was at, or was she okay. So many times, I wanted desperately to go to the police for help, but I was afraid they would take my little sister from me. My little sister was diagnosed with ADHD; she needed special attention. I would walk her to school every day; she never missed a day because I wanted more for her than myself. I would wash by hand the few clothes we had. I would wash and comb her hair. We were very young kids, but we did the best we could with what we had. At the time she was seven and I was eleven, my little sister was my world; she was the only somebody I had.

Reason why you are in juvenile: I started selling drugs to support my little sister and me. I remember when I made money, I would buy school supplies, clothes, food, and pay the rent. My only concern was my little sister; she is my world and she is innocent, just like me.

Tell what it's like in juvenile: I hate being here; but in a way, it saved my life. I promised myself to do better, get any education, and attend college. I want a better life for my baby sister and me.

What would you tell others to help them? No matter what you are going through, remember, it is not the end. If you had problems like I did, you know more than anyone what it's like to not have and what it's like to have parents that are not supportive. But you should also know your parents' problems are not yours, so don't blame yourself.

It is up to you to make your life better, and believe me you can do it. It's not hard; it's only hard when you make it hard. And don't look at your life as being difficult just because things have been hard for you; remember there are people in this world who had a rough childhood but are successful today because they wanted to change their life. If they can do it, guess what? You can do it as well.

Peer pressure: I don't believe in peer pressure because I'm not a bad person, and I'm not a follower. I only did what I had to do in order to survive; if I had to do it over, I would do things differently.

To parents: Don't forget you had us. We didn't have you; so be a parent. Remember that was a vow you made to God when we came into this world.

Karen
Age: 18

What it was like growing up? I grew up in foster care; my mother lost custody of me and my four siblings. My mother was on drugs ever since I was little. She would try for a couple of days to stop, but she couldn't stop; she was on heroin. I remember watching her inject her body with drugs; it was something I would never forget. She was in another world, her body was limp, and her eyes would roll into the back of her head; it was frightening. Many times, I wanted to end my life so I could end the pain; my life was like a dead end. I had no one to turn to for help. Why me? Why me? I would say, why me as I would pray for strength.

Reason why you are in juvenile: I ran away from my foster home at least four times; my foster mother was a nice person. I have nothing but respect for her. I thank her for allowing me to live with her, but she is not my mother. After everything I went through with my mother, I still miss her after all; she is the one who gave me life. I truly feel I can help her.

What is it like in juvenile? I don't like taking orders from anyone, but I have no other choice. I feel like I'm by myself; no one understands. I think I would be a better person if my mother was a part of my life. It doesn't matter if I have a good day or a bad day; I think about my mother constantly. I wonder if she thinks about me as well; one day, I will find her and all my troubles will be over.

Pregnancy: I got pregnant when I was fourteen; I love my daughter. I only wish I would have waited; my daughter is in foster care, and it's scary because it's like a cycle because my mother was also in foster homes when she was younger.

Peer pressure: I always tried to fit in with the crowd; I wanted to belong. I didn't feel worthy. I wish I were a stronger person. I cry all the time because I feel lost. especially not having my mother in my life. I know my life will get better because I refuse to throw my precious life away. This is the only life I will get; and if I don't make it happen, no one else will because I'm responsible for my own life.

To parents: You may feel as if we don't need you, and we don't love you. The bottom line is, we do need you, and yes, we do love you. Be a parent from the beginning to the end; get your life together before it's too late, before the love your child have for you turn into hate toward you.

Angela
Age: 17

What was it like growing up? I was raised by both parents; growing up was okay. We had lots of parties ever since I could remember almost every week. My parents had many friends; every day it was somebody different. I remember my parents got stone drunk; they both collapsed on the living room floor. I tried waking them, but they were knocked out. I went into my room. I was in the bed sleeping, and my father's best friend came into my room. When I woke up, he was next to me. One thing led to another; and before I knew it, we were having sex. I promised him I would not tell anyone, especially my parents. At the time, I was only thirteen. I really didn't know better. I was scared and ashamed. I felt dirty; how could I let this happen to me? I couldn't understand why I didn't scream for help or fight back; of course, I blamed myself. After the incident took place with my father's friend and me, I never was the same again. Deep down inside, I blamed my parents for allowing this man into our home. I was afraid to tell anyone, and I definitely couldn't tell my parents; there was no telling what my father would have done.

Reason why you are in juvenile: I got into a fight with this girl. I had to protect myself. So I hit her with pipe and broke her nose; her parents pressed charges, and I was sent away to juvenile.

What is it like in juvenile? Of course, I don't like it. Who would? Every day someone is fighting. When I see little girls, twelve years old, entering into the system, I really feel sorry for them because they can't defend themselves against the bigger girls.

What would you tell others to help them? I realize why I'm here, and I'm not ashamed to admit I was wrong. At first, I didn't care; if I had the chance, I would have done it again because I was defending myself. We had words, and from there, one thing led to another. I was wrong because I struck first; and when I really think about it, I could have killed or seriously injured that girl instead of sitting in juvenile. I could be sitting in jail serving some years at least fifteen or more. When you are in juvenile or jail, you spend a lot of time thinking about your past; you ask yourself over and over, was it worth it? Why put yourself in a situation where you're helpless and there is nothing you can do except wait on time to pass by? I'm locked up, and that girl is living her life. It makes no sense; and every time I think about it, I get angry with myself for letting it happen. The girl I was fighting didn't have a weapon, that's why she is living her life and I'm locked up. Some of the girls here have the I-don't-care attitude; the sad thing is they don't understand the pressure they are putting on themselves. If they don't wish to change, that's their problem; more than likely they will be back into the system. As young adults, we should be trying to do what is right, treat others as you would like to be treated. We don't have to be mad and angry toward one another and stop thinking everybody is your enemy. There are people out there who really want to see you succeed in life. Sometimes strangers pray a prayer for you; remember, they don't have to know you in order to pray for you. But because you show the Eve in you, you probably stopped your blessing.

KD
Age: 16

What was it like growing up? It was hell flat out; ever since I could remember, I have always been responsible and blamed for everything, from age three until now. Put it like this: my mother loved every man that came her way; the only problem was they didn't love her; they only used her. I saw my mother having sex with different guys, as if it was nothing to be ashamed of. When one man leaves, another comes. I had an older brother; he would actually fight the guys to keep them away from my mother. I remember this one guy punched my brother so hard in his stomach my brother fell to the floor trying to catch his breath. At the time, my brother was twelve and the man was probably in his thirties. My mother told my brother that she was going to whip his ass if he ever gets in her business; her favorite words were: I'm grown up, and you are a kid so stand in a kid's place. I guess she thought because we were young kids, we didn't have feelings; or our feelings didn't matter.

Reason why you are in juvenile: I joined a gang; they were my family, at least, I thought so.

Tell what it's like in juvenile: Man, this place is for the dogs; nobody cares about you or your feelings.

What would you tell others to help them? You are your only true friend, for real; and nobody, I mean nobody, will love you like you love yourself; so don't be fooled. Take pride in yourself. I had to learn the hard way, but you don't have to because I'm telling you. Don't think everybody is your friend because they say they are; pay close attention to how they treat you; see if they talk bad about you to other people; and mainly see if they will support you, especially if you are doing something positive. If not, they are not your friends, be aware, be very aware of who you call *friend*.

Peer pressure: All you need is one best friend; and if you can't find that, you don't need enemies.

Mary
Age: 17

What was it like growing up? What a joke! I never met my father; I don't even know if he is dead or alive. My mother's favorite words are; you act just like your father. I often wondered how is that, does he wear makeup, does he move his hips when he walk, or does he have feminine ways? No, I'm not perfect; I make mistakes like any normal person. But if my mother had anything to say, she would of course say only negative things about me. All my life, she did nothing but put me down, as if she blamed me for my father not being in my life or perhaps hers. The more I tried to be a daughter to my mother, the more she would pull away. I never understood. I guess I will never understand. She would not open up to me. My mother would always say that when I turn sixteen, she wanted me out of her house; I was still in school doing fairly good. My plans were to graduate from high school and go to college in another state so my mother wouldn't be bothered with me, especially since that's what she wanted.

Reason why you are in juvenile: Sure enough when I turned sixteen, my beloved mother told me I had to leave; I had no place to go. The very next day, I had an exam to take at school. I told my mother, or should I say I begged her, to please let me stay. She said no; I had to get out her house. My mother became very violent; she struck me extremely hard on the side of my face. I lost it; I punched her back. I had to defend myself; I had no idea what she was going to do next. She called the cops; when the police came, she told them I tried to kill her, and I threatened her. I couldn't understand why my mother would tell such a lie; she knows I was not going to hurt her. Why was she trying to destroy me?

What would you tell others to help them? Although I had a rough relationship with my mother, I will never let her unhappiness affect me. Even if I never see her again, I refuse to be like her. Life is too short, and I'm going to make the best of it while I can. Yes, I am angry with my mother for lying on me, which is why I'm in juvenile. I realize my mother's life is hers, and my life belongs to me. I'm seventeen now, and I know I will be okay because no one can make me happy but myself.

Peer pressure: If you were going through what I've been through, you would appreciate life a lot better. Peer pressure to me is just another word; to me, it means happiness.

Pregnancy: I am so glad I do not have kids. I know I'm ready for the responsibility. First, get yourself together, stay in school, and make something of your life. Don't cheat your child out of life; first, make something of yours so you can share it with your child. When you struggle, your child will struggle; and when you have, your child will have.

To parent: With everything I went through with my mother, I refuse to hate her because that would make me like her, and I refuse to be like her. When parents misuse a child, they never know how much joy a child can bring to them, until the child is no longer in their life. Mom, take care of yourself. I hope one day, you will be able to forgive yourself and make peace within yourself.

Diamond
Age: 17

What was it like growing up? I was molested when I was four years old by a relative. My mother was more like a friend than a mother. I called her by her first name. Because it was hard to call her mom; besides, she would tell me to call her by her first name, especially when we were out in public; my mother was older than the man she dated. Growing up was difficult because I didn't have a role model. When I was molested, I never forgot that incident; the pain is deep down in my soul. I could be wrong, but I don't think my mother would have cared if I was molested. My mother, or should I say Kay, was not the kind of mother who took things seriously. Her concern was not on me. Sometimes she would boldly ask some of my classmate's parents if I could stay the night or weekend with them because she wanted to go out. It was so embarrassing; some of the kids I barely knew.

Reason why you are in juvenile: I dropped out of school when I was fifteen. I would stay out sometimes until the next morning or sometimes longer. Kay had me locked up. I guess so she wouldn't have to be bothered with me anymore.

What is it like in juvenile? Put it like this, I don't ever want to come back here ever. Imagine being locked in your house for one year, and you can't get out. Every day you see the same faces of people you really don't like, or sharing a room with someone you don't like because that's exactly how it is.

What would you tell others to help them? If you have a parent or parents whom you know love you and want what is best for you, you don't know how blessed you really are. Imagine living the life I had with a mother who didn't love you and a father whom you never met. You should get on your knees every night; thank the almighty God for blessing you with a mother or father to love you.

You may not know this, but there are so many kids in this world that has nobody to love or care for them. I'm one of them. So what if your parents stay on your back about doing the right thing; so what if they don't want you to hang around with the wrong crowd of people because if they didn't care, they wouldn't say anything. So stop with the attitude and accept the blessing God has giving you because if you don't, God can remove them from your life. Why do you think he should keep blessing you, and you're not grateful? Do you realize you are nothing compared to God? Everything you say or do, he is looking down on you; so don't take it for granted.

If you think you don't need your parents, think again. Please, I ask you if for any reason you are angry or have bitterness toward your parents for any reason, make peace with them; remember, tomorrow is not promised to any of us, young or old. Just look around you, you read about it in the paper, and you see on television; every day people's lives are taken. There are thirty girls in my facility; nine of the girls' relatives had died since they were being locked up, three lost their mother, two lost their father, one lost her sister, and three of the girls' brothers were killed. Find it in your heart to love; but first of all, love and respect yourself.

Peer pressure: Stay away from people who are trouble; people who are trouble mean you no good. They are not honest, trustworthy friends because they don't understand what it means. Just think about it, how can a person who is a negative, troubled person have respect and love for anyone? It's impossible; either you are a negative person or a positive person. Surround yourself with people who respect themselves because they are the ones who respect and mean good for others. It took this to happen to me before I understood. Since I'm being locked up, I got my GED, and I will be taking up a trade when I leave.

To parents: Remember, your children are a product of you. Whatever you do or say can and usually will affect them. So don't blame anyone but yourself for not setting values and mortals for them. If you're trashy and no good, more than likely they will be the exact same way because they learned it from you. If you're a good parent with values and morals, more than likely they will have values and mortal because learned it from you.

Tone
Age: 17

What was it like growing up? Growing up for me was not good at all. My parents were together, but they fought all the time. My father owns a successful business; my mother was an accountant. To me, it didn't matter about what I had or the things I had; those things are material things. Of course, when you're young, it's beautiful; but as you start getting older, you see things differently. My father was very controlling; if things didn't go his way, all hell would break loose. I got feed up with all his crap. I was really mad at my mother for staying; she didn't have to take that. She had a decent job paying pretty good money. Every time they would fight, I mean fight, she would be crying, telling him she was going to leave. Of course, I was happy; but in a couple of days, she would forget. She said it; eventually when she would say it, I stop believing her. I have four siblings, and we all were tired of my father and his controlling ways. Sometimes I had to go to work with him; he would fuss and call me names in front of his employees. He didn't care; man, he was straight out cold. I remember this one time he called me stupid, and I couldn't be his son because I wasn't ambitious like him; I was only a kid. One of his female employees told him he was disrespectful and rude. He was shocked because nobody ever told him that, or should I say talk to him in that way, especially an employee. I don't think she cared if she got fired because she was really upset.

Reason why you are in juvenile: I joined a gang mainly to get away from my father. He always talked bad about me anyway, so I gave him a real reason to down-rate me.

What is it like in juvenile? The truth, it's rough; your life is in their hands. Every day it's the same old thing; you feel like a criminal, and they treat you like you are.

What would you tell others to help them? It's bad when you express yourself and people don't listen. Some people take things in a joking way when you are dead serious, and I am dead serious when I say this. Don't get caught up in the bullshit, point blank. People, especially teenagers, don't take life seriously because we haven't experienced a lot of things. I'm not talking about sex or drugs; those are negative things. I'm speaking about the good things in life, and the only way we will find out is if we get an education, stay focused, and be determined to make our life better. No, I'm not saying everybody is college material because you don't need a college degree in order to be successful. But what you do need in order to be successful or in order to make something good of your life is to stay focused and not let anyone influence you to go backward. Don't let some confused lowlife stop you from being the best you can be. Listen, I don't care if you are an A student or a D student; you are still somebody, and you can make the best of your life, but you have to want it. Don't wait on somebody to give it to you because if you do, you will never get it. If I don't get my ass together by the time I leave this place, I'm in trouble because I know my father is not going to help me. I got my GED; and when I leave, I'm taking up a trade so I can get a descend paying job, and then I'm going to college to get my degree. The bottom line is it's up to you to change your life so you can have a better life.

Just because your parents or your family struggled in life does not mean you have to struggle. Don't be so hard on yourself; give yourself a chance to succeed. Take advantage of every opportunity that can help you become a better person. I don't care how rough your life was or how easy your life was; don't use it as an excuse to not want anything better for you.

Peer pressure: Be selective in everything you do, even with friends.

To parents: It's not healthy for any parent to keep their kids in an abusive surrounding just because you choose to stay in one.

Joyce
Age: 18

What was it like growing up? I was the eldest of five children; we all had different fathers. My father was an ex-con; he was in prison, basically, my whole life. My mother is on welfare and has been my whole life. My mother said the more children you have, the more money you will get on welfare; this was something she would tell my little sister and me all the time. I started dating when I was twelve, I got pregnancy when I was thirteen. My mother was so happy she was going to become a grandmother. I wanted to have an abortion, but she said I couldn't. I believe my mother only wanted me to keep my baby so I could be on welfare like her. I wanted to stay in school, but my mother said she was not going to watch my baby; she suggested it would be better if I stay home, so I dropped out of school.

I now have three children, and I'm not proud to admit, but I am also receiving welfare. All three of my babies' daddies promised me that we were going to get married, but it never happened, as a matter of fact, they don't spend any time with my children. Two of my babies' dads I have not seen them in over one year. I have no idea where they are or how to find those bums.

Reason why you are in Juvenile: I got caught selling drugs; I know it's wrong, but I had to make money to support my babies.

What is it like in juvenile? It's hard because you have to deal with these different attitudes these girls have. They wake up with an attitude, and they go to bed with one.

What would you tell others to help them? If I had a chance to live my life over, I would be the happiest person in the world. Yes, I love my kids, but this is not the life I would choose. The first thing I would want different, and I'm sorry to say it, but it's the truth, and that is a different mother. I want a mother who is loving, respectful, and successful, a mother who has morals and values because then my life would be different, or should I say better. I'm not blaming my mother for the choices I've made; but if she would have showed me or talked to me about life I know, I would not have three babies.

Calvin
Age: 17

What was it like growing up? Growing up in my house was okay, I guess; my mother was black and my father was white. Being biracial didn't bother me; although it bothered some people, to me, they had the problem, not me. My mother was strict; my father was a hard worker. He took care of everything; my mother stayed home to care for my sibling and me. My mother had a problem with every person I hung around; she didn't like anyone. She said they were trouble, but it really was true. As a matter of fact, one of my best friends graduated from high school with high honors and went to college.

Reason why you are in juvenile: I started getting high trying to fit in with the crowd. I begin using just about any kind of drugs you could think of, even heroin. I started stealing from my parents first; and later, I started breaking into people homes searching for money or things to sales to support my habit. I knew it was wrong, but I didn't care because I had a problem; I was addicted to drugs.

What is it like in juvenile? I feel like I'm trapped in a small room, and I can't get out, especially in the summer when you can't go outside to hang out with your friends; it's tough.

What would you tell others to help them? If you are doing wrong, it's not worth it. Once you are caught, your freedom is gone; when you enter into the juvenile system, you have no idea how long you will be in the system. Usually it's one to three years, depending on the crime; and if you have previous crimes against you, sometimes it can be longer.

Peer pressure: The one thing I am so mad about is the fact that my best friend had more sense than I did. When I started doing drugs, I changed. I couldn't control my behavior. My best friend stopped dealing with me completely. I can't blame him for that because I would have done the exact same thing if it were him. Now he is in college and I'm in juvenile. I'm sure he is doing just great; I wish I could say the same thing about myself. The one thing I would like to say is stay focused and do the right thing.

To parents: Be a good parent. You don't have to be rich in order to be a good parent. Just talk to your child all the time even if they don't want to hear it because the more you tell them, the more they will understand. And don't be so strict because once they get in their teens, they are going to try even more to experience a lot of different things, and it may not be what you want.

Tisha
Age: 17

What was it like growing up? Growing up for me was not good. I really don't have any good memories. My mother was always involved with different men. I remember meeting this guy for the first time; the second time I met him, he was moving in with us. I couldn't remember his name because I met him only once. My mother said he was staying with us because he had no place to go; in other words, he was homeless. I believe my mother liked him because he was handsome. I didn't trust him because he would always look at me really strange. I stayed over my friend's house most of the time. How could my mother allow some strange person live with us whom she knew nothing about?

Reason why you are in juvenile: I started prostituting.

What is it like in juvenile? I don't like it. I would rather be in the streets than in here.

What would you tell others to help them? I have nothing to say; let them find out the hard way like I did.

Peer pressure: If people wish to be stupid, then be a follower. I'm not a follower. I just did something I should not have done.

To parents: Don't sleep with every man or woman you see and expect for your child to respect you. There are certain things we as children don't forget.

Tina
Age: 17

What was it like growing up? I really hate talking about my childhood; although my psychologist said I need to talk about it in order to release the anger. I was raped by my uncle and his friend when I was twelve; although he was not my real uncle, my mother was dating his brother. My mother's boyfriends raped me as well; they said I was developed like a mature woman. My mother found out, and would you believe she still married that child molester? My real father was deceased. Ever since I was nine years old, my stepfather raped me at least six times; I was removed from my house into foster care at the age of fourteen. No one wanted me, and no one wanted to adopt me. I don't label myself as a bad person. I just wanted to fit in and be accepted for once in my life.

Reason why you are in juvenile: I got involved with a gang for all the wrong reason. I was looking for some attention and protection. I got into a fight with some girls; we all had weapons.

What is it like in juvenile? I feel lost. I have no visits; no one cares, but I will get through this and become a better person. All I want is to be happy for a change.

What can you tell others to help them? Believe in yourself. Don't let anyone bring you down. Even though I don't have anyone to care for me, I know God love me more than I could love myself. I'm a rape victim at first, I was bitter. I hated myself, my mother and all the men who took my virginity; they will no longer take away my dignity. With therapy, I come to realize that my body is my temple, and I will do my best to be the best.

Peer pressure: Hang around people who want something because they are the people who will do right by you. Don't become friends with people who are doing wrong; believe me, they won't have your back no matter what they promise you.

To parents: You know I didn't have a mom to care about me, and I paid the price for it, and I believe, one day, she will need me for something, and I won't be there to rescue her. I truly believe what goes around comes around. Don't be like my mother; love your child and be a friend to your child, but first be a parent because we need you more than you can imagine.

Carl
Age: 17

How was it growing up? I was the only child; my mother was an alcoholic and on with heroin. She left me alone for days and sometimes nights; my grandparents died. I had one aunt, and she lived in another state. My mother was not a bad mother, but she was sick. The few times when she was drug free, she made sure I had food, shelter, and clothing; but when she was getting high, nothing else matter, not even me. I remembered completing my homework assignments by myself at a very early age. I was probably six or seven; sometimes it was completed and sometimes it wasn't. Her boyfriend tried to be a father to me; he was also an alcoholic. I started selling drugs to pay the rent; I was fourteen.

Reason why you are in juvenile: I sold drugs to the wrong person.

What is it like in juvenile? It's hard. I wish I was any place but here.

What can you tell others to help them? I pray that no child live the life I lived, although I know there are kids that are walking in my shoes. Stay in school; no matter what, work hard if that's what it takes. Since I've been locked up, my mother passed away. I never got a chance to tell her I loved her and that I forgive her because I know she was a sick person. Although I'm still hurt inside, apart of her still lives within me. I'm by myself now; I have no family and no friends. I pray all the time for strength and guidance. The sad thing about some folks is no matter what hard times they experienced in their life, they will never learn. They are constantly in and out of trouble with the law until eventually, they wind up in jail for a much serious crime because they don't take life seriously and they don't appreciate the beauty of life.

Peer pressure: Stand strong and believe in yourself; do not get involved with negative people. If they are doing wrong, let them do it by themselves; don't become their slaves.

To parents: We depend on you for everything, and if you're not there for us, who will be? My mother is no longer with me; she chose drugs over her life. If you are doing drugs and you truly want to stop, you can. To be honest, you cause us more pain than you cause yourself; and for those parents who are doing drugs, instead of being a parent, you are selfish and wrong. We did nothing to you, so why hurt us; and if you think you're not, believe me you are actually killing us.

Kimberly
Age: 17

What was it like growing up? I lived with my father and four siblings; my mother left my father and us. She never came to visit or called us. Her mother, my grandmother, said she would call from time to time; but she didn't bother to contact us. My father married my stepmother when I was eight years old. She is more like a mother than my mother could ever be. My father was involved with my education as well as my stepmother; growing up was not so bad.

Reason why you are in juvenile: I started hanging out with the wrong people who basically did everything under the sun. They were definitely a bad influence for me; they were into sex and wild parties. I started hanging out coming in at two and three o'clock in the morning; my father said I was out of control and called the cops. He turned me over to juvenile just like that. I couldn't believe my father and stepmother. I hated them for that.

What is it like in juvenile? I don't like being here. I stay in fights to defend myself; the girls here are trouble, looking for anyone to pick on. When you come to a place like this, you have to defend yourself or else. These two girls got into a fight; one picked up an object and busted the girl in her head. The girl who got a busted head did nothing to deserve that. So before you get in trouble, think about defending yourself because that's how it is.

What would you tell others to help them? You better start obeying your parents; if you're not, they may not punish you in any other way, but they can make a call to the police if you are out of control and turn you over to juvenile. There are girls here at this facility that are locked up because they were out of control; it happens all the time.

Pregnancy: Don't have a child because your girlfriend has one or you are trying to hold on to some guy. The best way to hold on to a guy is to keep your head on straight.

Peer pressure: I am the prime example of peer pressure. I started hanging out with a group of girls and boys who skipped school. We partied and hung out smoking cigarette, drinking, getting high. At the time, I didn't see anything wrong with it. Don't get involved with people who don't want anything and don't have respect for anyone, especially themselves. Being locked up, I see clearly the mistakes I made; and my father was not going to let me get away with that. One of the girls whom I hung out with got killed. It's not like she was a bad person; she made bad decisions. If your parent tells you if you don't straighten up, something bad may happen to you, please listen to their advice. The one girl who was killed, her mother told her that all the time, she even told us, but she didn't listen. I often cry when I think about her. Remember, you don't have to put yourself through the trouble. Take care of yourself and do the right thing; when I get out of here, I know I'm going to college or take a trade so I can be a better person. I know I don't know you, but I love you because I understand what you are going through because I was in your shoes. Please stop doing wrong before it's too late.

To parents: Thank God for good parents. Respect and take care of your parent, and you will live a happier life. I finally realize that now. Dad and Mom, I'm sorry; I know you meant well.

Larry
Age: 17

What was it like growing up? I was a kid who was never happy; my father was abusive to my mother. He would call her some of the worse name you could think of h—, b—everything, it was terrible. The sad thing I never forgot; I hated my father. Man, I wanted to hurt him for all the pain he caused my mother and my siblings. He was really hard on the boys; we suffered more than my sisters did. All I could remember was wanting to do bodily harm to this mean person; the thought of him, actually being my father, made me sick to my stomach.

Reason why you are in juvenile: I started selling drugs, and I dropped out of school.

What is it like in juvenile? Juvenile is no different from being in jail; to me, it's all the same. The only thing that is different is the age. There are some guys in here that are going straight to jail when they turn eighteen years old. I pray and hope I'm not one of them.

What would you tell others to help them? Whatever you do, don't start selling drugs; no matter what, get a job in a restaurant or wash cars; believe me it's worth it. I saw two guys get killed for drugs; it blew my mind. I was hiding; they didn't see me, I guess by the grace of God. Soon after that, I was caught; I guess I was one of the lucky ones.

Peer pressure: We discuss peer pressure every Friday, and what I realize is that peer pressure is only a word; no matter what, you are accountable for your action.

There is no judge in the world that will drop any charges because of peer pressure. You have to realize that we all have run into difficult times in this life, but it is entirely up to us to make the right decision. If I can do it, believe me, you can too; every night, get on your knees and pray, ask God to help you change to be a better person, and do the right thing. I do it every night, and I know I'm a changed person.

To parents: To all the dads out there, take care of your family, don't beat and misuse your wife or kids. Whatever you are going through, talk about it with your wife; your kids are innocent. We are not the cause for your problem. My father passed away from an illness he suffered from two years before he passed away. Not one of his kids were there for him, no one cared; my mother was with him to the end. The last thing he said was you really do love me. My mother is a good women and mother. A man who fights with his wife is a coward. I had more respect for a homeless man than my so-called father. If there were two men that needed to be rescued and one was my father, I would have saved the other man without a doubt. What a parent doesn't realize is when you cause pain to your family, that pain stays with them forever. You don't forget; sometimes it gets worse. So to all those so-called fathers and mothers, whoever, remember, whatever you do, it will come back on you.

Summer
Age: 17

What was it like growing up? I thought it was normal; I thought it was okay to be sexually active with your father. I thought it was okay for your mother to watch, and your brother and sisters to join in. My father molested us almost every day; sometimes we all did it, and sometimes we all took turns. My father would let his friends have sex with us for money so he could pay his bills. Sometimes we would go home with them or to a motel if they were married, and sometimes we stayed home. When my brother turned fourteen, he went to the police after the child protective service got involved, thank God. We were rescued, and my parents were sent to jail, and we went in foster care.

Reason why you are in juvenile: I started prostituting; something I was accustomed to, and the one thing I was good at.

What is it like in juvenile? I feel like my parents have won because I am locked up. I have no freedom; it's like being at home. I hate it here, and I hate home.

Pregnancy: I have two twin boys; although they are adopted, I still think about them. It was definitely the right thing to do, giving them up for adoption. Getting pregnant was a mistake; it was not planned. I don't know who my babies' daddies are, and I'm glad I don't.

Peer pressure: You don't need friends, especially if they are not on the same level you're on.

To parents: You are the ones who are supposed to protect us from harm, keep us safe, and not hurt us. If you have parents who love and protect you, believe me, you are blessed, and you should be grateful; put yourself in my shoes.

Carolyn
Age: 17

What was it like growing up? My aunt raised me from the age of nine. My parents were into illegal things; they were in and out of trouble, constantly, with the law. My aunt came to my parent's home and told them she was going to remove my little sister and me from the house, or she would call the authority on them; they didn't try to stop her because they knew she was serious. When my father went to jail, my mother begins to straighten up her life; she begins working, and she took up a trade in the medical field. She came and got my sister and me, and we begin living with her; I was fifteen years old at the time. I had so much anger toward my mother; what she said or did for me was not enough. I did things just to upset her because I was very angry because she treated my sister and me like clap when we were younger. This particular day, we actually got into a fight; she called the authorities on me, and I had to go to juvenile.

Reason why you are in juvenile: I was out of control and disrespectful toward my mother.

What is it like in juvenile? I have a problem with following orders, and that's all you do when you are in a place like this.

What would you tell others to help them? No matter how hard it may be, always do what your parents say, especially if they are right; do it so you won't be in a place like this. All it take is one call to the authority, and you will find yourself right here. And you can't leave when you want; it is up to the judge to make that decision if you are ready. I have been here for two years; my mother said I cannot come home. So when I leave here, I don't know where they will send me. My little sister is in high school getting good grades; she said she is going to college.

Peer pressure: Don't give in to peer pressure; my sister and I both went through the same thing with our parents not being there for us. My sister decided to do what was right; she didn't hang out with the wrong crowd. She kept focus; she has one year to go before she graduates and go on to college. I on the other hand, did the opposite and look where I am. I know I'm not college material; my grades were always bad. I know when I do leave this place, I will be taking up a trade so I can get a good job.

To parents: Talk to your children, spend family time with them, start when they are small. Remember, we don't stay little forever. Guide them and show them the right way; surround them with positive people. As parents, make sure your friends are the right people for your child to be around; it is important as well. If you have family members or friends that are not good example for your child, please don't allow those kinds of people around your child. Let them know why if you need to so they can understand; tell them why they are special. I believe, to love your child, is the number one ultimate goal.

Brian
Age: 17

What was it like growing up? I had two other sibling; they were adopted. I never met them; I know nothing about them. My mother was in and out of mental institution; she could not care for me like a mother could care for a child. My father had custody of me; he wasn't much of a father himself. I remember when we were getting evicted from a one-bedroom apartment; it was filthy with rats and mice throughout the entire apartment building, drug addicts and drunks surrounding the building. This particular day, my father asked me to go to the store to buy a can of rice soup; as I was walking down the street, I realized I had no money. I was twelve years old at the time. I ran back home to get the money from my father; as I approached the door, I heard a gunshot. I called for my father, but he didn't answer. He was in the bathroom; he shot himself. I called out his name, but he didn't answer. I watched him die slowly; his eyes started rolling in the back of his head. It seems as if he was trying to say good-bye. From that moment on, I realized I was by myself in a world I knew nothing about. I didn't know how to get help or where to find help. I ran to a park where I slept for days. I saw kids with their mom and dad. I wanted so much to go to them for help, but I couldn't. I thought they were going to push me away. I cried and cried and cried, but I had no more tears; all I had was a broken heart, not even a penny in my pocket. It started raining. I watched people leave the park in their cars; some walked and some rode their bikes. Everyone was gone, even the squirrels vanished. I sat on the bench with only my pants, shirt, and shoes on. I was afraid to go back to the apartment. After the rained stopped, two officers were driving in the park; they walked over to me and ask what was I doing out. I was terrified, but I had to tell them the truth. I wanted someone to save me. The officers took me to the station, and from there, I went to foster care.

Reason why you are in juvenile: I was in and out of foster homes. I joined a gang for all the wrong reasons I wanted to belong.

What is it like in juvenile? I really feel lost. I have no family members that come to see or write me.

What would you tell others to help them? If you have a mother or father or even a relative who love you and want the best for you, believe me, you really don't realize how bless you are. Imagine living my life; if any body should be bitter or even angry at the world, it should be me, but you know I'm not. I realize things in our lives happen for a reason, and everybody deals a different hand for one purpose. Since I've been in this facility, I got my GED. I feel like the world has lifted off my shoulder, why I can't explain. I hope my story will help you realize how blessed you really are; and if you are going through hard times with your parent, remember there is someone out there who is going through something harder than you. This is a tough world and no one owes you anything, not even your parents. If your heart is good and you have respect for yourself and others, your blessings are just around the corner, just hold on and believe and dream big.

Peer pressure: I know I joined the gang for all the wrong reasons; it was a big mistake, and I am paying a price for it. Don't let my mistake be your mistake; graduate from high school or get your GED and make something out of your life. The life my parents lived can very well become yours if you don't make the best of it. Keep your head on straight and don't let anyone stop you from a future.

To parents: I didn't have a mother to care for me; and as you know from reading my story, my father also had problems. Please take care of your children to the best of your ability. Set examples for your children, get involved; just a couple of hours a day can make a big difference.

SUCCESSFUL TEENAGERS

Similar Lifestyles Teens Tell Their Stories and
Why They Refuse to Let Anything Stop Them

August
Age: 16

What was it like growing up? I grew up in single home; my mother was a waitress in a restaurant. On weekends, she would always tell my two sisters and me that the weekends was her time to have fun. She was never involved in any of our school activities or homework. I remember many times not completing my homework because I needed help. I was honest with my teacher. I told her my mother would not help me. Because I did fairly well in class, I was able to keep my grades up. Of course, it bothers me not to have my mother involved in any of my school activities; several of my friends' parents and relatives would always support them; as a matter of fact, they never once met my mother. I'm sure people thought I didn't have a mother because she was not involved in any of my school activities; she never met any of my teachers.

What would you tell others to help them? Keep pushing yourself to do what is right; as you know, my mother didn't spent time with my sisters and me; we had to learn things on our own. Basically, we support each other.

Peer pressure: Whatever you do, do not surround yourself with negative people, especially if things are not going right at home, because it will only make things worse. I do understand what you are going through; sometimes we feel like we are by ourselves, and people don't understand us when actually we don't need anyone to make us feel important or comfort us. All we need is ourselves.

Pregnancy: I have a boyfriend whom I see from time to time; he realizes how important education is to me. I may not be the smartest person in the world, but I am someone who wants something out of life. I will never depend on anyone to give me anything because once you depend on someone to give you or take care of you, they will feel as if they own you. I have my own mind, and I refuse to let anyone tell me what I can or cannot do.

To parents: Be involved with your child's school activities and homework assignments, encourage them to do what is right.

Leeza
Age: 17

What was it like growing up? I was raised by my father; my mother was on drugs, and she had nothing to do with me. My father was involved with women who had no interest in me. Being the only child, it was rough, but I refuse to let my father and his relationship become my problem. Instead, I started participating in different academic activities in school.

What would you tell others to help them? Just because you are not happy with your situation at home, don't add to the problem, and don't become the problem; stay focused, aim high, and before you know it, you made it through.

Pregnancy: There is nothing wrong with wanting to have a baby, but wait until you finish high school, attend college, or a trade at least; that way, you will be able to support yourself and your baby. You won't have to depend on anyone, or welfare.

Peer pressure: I had to deal with peer pressure and so did a lot of us. I had friends or should I say associates come and ask me to get involved with things that were illegal, but I refused, and of course they stopped speaking to me. To be honest, I was glad; life is too short. So why would anyone want to waste it? Make the best of it; enjoy life to the fullest. Stay away from troubled people; believe me, they don't mean you any good. The only thing they enjoy is staying in trouble and causing trouble for no reason at all. Before you know it, life will pass them by, and they will find themselves homeless or on drugs. Majority of the people you see on the streets that are homeless or on drugs started out as teenagers.

To parents: It is so important that you support us, especially if we are doing are best in whatever it is; encourage us and support us.

Darren
Age: 17

What was growing up like? I was raised by my grandmother, my mother was on drugs, and my father was in prison for murder. Ever since I could remember, my mother had always been on drugs. I never met my father, and to be honest, I care not to. Knowing the life he led is enough for me. My grandmother did a pretty good job raising me the best she could. At least, I can honestly say she tried her best on a fixed income of $700.00 a month.

What would tell others to help them? For those who have walked in my shoes, you understand the pain and hurt of being abandoned by a parent; it was twice as hard for me because I was the only child. I had no one to talk to about my pain, only by grandmother. School was important to me as well as getting involved in school academics. Whatever you do, believe in yourself because you are not by yourself.

Peer pressure: If things in your life are not going right, and you are dealing with pain and hurt, please don't give up because it will get better. It is very important that you surround yourself with positive peers because more than likely they will help you through this. Once you surround yourself with negative people, your problems will only get worse. The pain and hurt you are feeling will grow into anger, and once anger set in trouble will follow you, or you will find yourself in trouble.

To parents: If you are a parent that is on drugs or alcohol, please keep in mind that you are to blame for your child's anger and pain because you choose to live the life you are living. How dare you try to give your child any advice when you caused the problem. Get it to together before the problem you caused become a bigger problem. To my peers, I understand what you are going through, and together we will pull through this.

Angela
Age: 17

What was it like growing up? I am the youngest of two, my mother raised us by herself, and my father was married with three other children; at the time when he and my mother were dating, he was not married. My father was in and out of my life; his biggest concern was his other family. Although he lived twenty minutes away from me, it didn't matter to him, and I was not his concern. My mother dropped out of school when she was fifteen years old. She got pregnant when she was fourteen; times have always been hard on my mother and us. My mother has always worked; but because she didn't graduate or have a trade, the job she had never paid enough. I can remember many times not having the clothes or things I wanted because my mother couldn't afford it; my mother said my father promised her that he would marry her, but he changed his mind after he found another woman who had no children. My mother and father were friends from the age of twelve; they thought they were in love until I was born. My mother said the biggest mistake was listening to all the promises he made to her.

What would you tell others to help them? At first, not having my father in my life bothered me a great deal; everybody wants both of their parents to love them. Girls especially want their dads. Once I started believing in me and loving myself, I didn't care if my father chose not to have me in his life because it's his loss, not mine. If he never came around me, it was okay with me. School became my solutions, instead of my problem. I surround myself with peers who know what they want out of life; so if you are looking for friends, take your time to find the right friends.

Peer pressure: Remember, my mother was a product of peer pressure; she was pressured into having my brother. My father promised her he would be there for her; and once I was born, he realized having a family was too much so he packed his bags and left. He never came back; my mother suffered and struggled because he promised her he was going to be there for her. Don't let peer pressure control you; you control it. Keep looking straight ahead and aim high because you deserve all of what life has to offer and more.

To parents: You know we didn't ask to be born, and we don't deserve to be hurt; so please help us so we can become respectable young adults.

Carmen
Age: 15

What was it like going up? Growing up in my house was very difficult; my mother had five kids, and we all had different fathers. My mother was involved with different men. Ever since I could remember, she wanted us to call them daddy. My sister's father is a married man. Sometimes he comes to visit, but she never went to his house to visit him because his wife knows nothing about my sister. He and his wife have been married for twenty-eight years; he has three other kids whom my sister never met. My mother has never set rules for us; my two brothers are in and out of trouble, constantly. The hardest problem I have is having a mother who has no interest in what I do.

What would you tell others to help them? To my peers, keep reaching for higher and better things in life. Sometimes you might have to distance yourself from certain friends and family members. It's not that you think of yourself as being better than your family or friends, but you sometimes in order to achieve your goals, your mind must be focused.

Peer pressure: Let's get real; peer pressure is a part of life because it exists. You don't have to be a part of it; nobody can make you do something you wish not to do. You do it because you want to.

To parents: It is up to parents to not put their child in an uncomfortable atmosphere; be a role model and teach your child respect for themselves and others.

Roger
Age: 17

What was it like growing up? I was raised in and out of foster homes; my parents were very abusive. Both were on drugs, heroin as a matter of fact. My siblings were adopted; they were younger than I was. I have not seen my brothers and sister since then, twelve years ago. Growing up in and out of foster homes was tough. I never felt wanted. I felt like no one loved me; it was really hard. I can remember staying with different families. I would get used to a family; and before you knew it, I was staying with a different family. I could never understand why no family would adopt me; all I ever wanted was a family. I became very angry and bitter with everyone.

What would you tell others to help them? Growing up in and out of foster homes was extremely hard for me. I was angry and bitter because I felt as if no one loved me. Until one day, when I was coming from school, and this homeless man was sitting at the bus stop were I was going to catch the bus, he asked me for a quarter. He was smelling so bad you could smell him a mile away. His teeth had turned black, the few he had. His hair was tangled and dirty. His clothes and shoes had holes everywhere. He had a rope around his waist to hold his pants up. While sitting at the bus stop, I had time to thank and tell God I was blessed because my life was nothing compared to this homeless man; not once did I laugh or think less of this man, because this man could very well be me one day if I kept thinking little of myself. I realized at that very moment I was worth something, and my life was what I make it to be. I start improving my grades from Ds to Bs. It was hard, but I did it. I set plans and goals for myself. This is my last year in high school. I will be attending college in the fall. This is the only life I will have, and I'm going to live it to the best of my ability. The boy who never had a home or a family to love him is now a young man who is dreaming big and reaching high.

Peer pressure: Peer pressure is nothing compared to what I lived through. If peer pressure came knocking at my door ten times each time I would be able to handle it. But if being homeless like the man I saw at the bus stop came knocking one time, it would be one time to many. Don't let anyone talk you into doing wrong, make your own decisions, and I promise you, you will be damn glad you did try it. Just say *no* to all the wrong things and *yes* to all the right things.

To parents: I know when the day comes when I get married and have children. I will be the best father I could ever be because I know what it's like to feel like to be not loved. To all the parents, I ask you, I beg you to be the best parent you could ever be because that seed you plant will one day multiply.

Gina
Age: 16

What was it like growing up? My father raised my sister and me; my mother died when I was six years old from drugs. My father worked and sold drugs for a living; he worked odd jobs to cover up his drug business. My sister and I only had each other because my father showed little interest in our lives. I often wonder why he didn't give us away for adoption. I'm sure it wouldn't been any worse. It was a summer day in June; my sister and I were sleeping. I remember my sister getting out of the bed; the next thing I heard were gunshots. I saw my sister lying on the floor; she was shot. She died instantly from a gunshot. Earlier that day my father got into a argument with some guy over drugs; later that night, he came back and shot the house up. I was twelve years old; my little sister was ten. My best friend was taken away from me. I couldn't believe my mother and little sister both are gone. I thought I would die; at least it would have been easier than to suffer the way I did.

What would you tell others to help them? If you are having any problems at home or at school, or if you are not happy for some reason, remember it will get better. Every last one of us has or had some problems in our lives; look at what I went through. Remember, I had no one, no family, and no friends. I was by myself, I grieved by myself, and I cried by myself; to make things worse, my father continued to sell drugs, and I had to stay in that same house thinking about my little sister constantly. The only thing help me was school; it was my only way out. I am an average student. I never made the honor roll; but at least, I tried, and I am still trying. My best friend and I both decided to go to college to make the best of our lives. I can honestly say that I feel like I am somebody, and nobody can tell me that I'm not. In order for things in your life to get better, please stay positive; make plans for your life. If you don't go to college, at least take up a trade; do something that will improve your life. Remember, you can do anything if you set your mind to it.

Peer pressure: Surround yourself with positive peers because then you won't have room for anything that is negative.

To parents: It's wrong to jeopardize your child's life because you wish to screw up your life. It's wrong to involve your child into your negative lifestyle. It's wrong to teach your child no values. It's wrong to misuse and abuse your child. It's wrong to inflict pain upon your child. And it's wrong to be anything other than a parent.

Fred
Age: 17

What was it like growing up? My parents divorced when I was seven years old; my father remarried. The summer months, I lived with my father; and during school year, I lived with my mother. My mother worked two jobs in order to pay bills; sometimes I stayed with my aunt; and sometimes I stayed with her male cousin. He started molesting me when I was eight years old. I never told my mother or father because he threatens me and told me what he would do to me if I did. Of course, I knew it wrong, but I was scared. I didn't know exactly what he would do. When I turned ten, I told my mother. I didn't care anymore; I was tired. All I wanted was for it to end; my mother was so mad that she went to my uncle and confronted him. She actually wanted to kill him after she left my uncle; she went to the authorities, and they arrested my uncle. I was proud of myself for the first time in two years. I felt like the world had lifted off my shoulders.

What would you tell others to help them? First of all, nobody has the right to touch you or hurt you; so don't think or feel as if it's your fault because it's not. If it was your fault, you won't be the victim; it's only your fault if you don't tell. So when they say don't tell or else, actually they mean tell or else. No, I'm not gay because of what happened to me. I'm very athletic, and I love the company of a young lady. So to all the young men who unfortunately went through this, never change who you are because if you do, they win. No, I am not a bitter person; actually, I put it behind me. My mother's cousin was sentenced to fifteen years in prison. I enjoy school; it helped me get through all the pain and hurt because it took my mind off my problems. Don't become the problem; become the solution, and the only way that can happen is if you keep your head on straight.

Peer pressure: Don't get involved with others who are in and of trouble; remember, if you surround yourself with people who are trouble, you will find yourself in trouble, more than likely with the law or dead. It's your choice and your decision.

To parents: If your child comes to you for help, please listen and help them. You are their hero and their strength; without you, we are lost.

Becky
Age: 17

What was it like growing up? I was raised with an alcoholic mother; my mother would drink in the morning, afternoon, and night. There were many times when I didn't go to school because my mother was too drunk to send me to school. She would lie in bed with a bad hang over. There were many alcoholics and drug addicts that stayed in our building. They would come over all the time; it was disgusting. The only thing that helped me was school. I knew this was not the life I wanted to live. I wanted no parts of this lifestyle, and the only way I would not enter into that lifestyle was to finish high school and go to college.

What would you tell others? Just because you are surrounded by drug addicts or alcoholics, you don't have to become part of that world; and in order not become part of that world, you must stay in school. Get your diploma no matter how hard it may be. Find a teacher you can talk to and let him know how you feel, be honest; they will help you if that's what you truly want.

I can't believe the time has come for me to graduate; and from there, I will be leaving to go on to college for a better future. If I can do it, believe me you can too.

Peer pressure? Of course, I had peers come to me and asked me to skip school, even get high with them. I couldn't see myself being that stupid. Being raised around my mother and her friends was enough for me not to want to live a life like that. I was not going to be caught up in that; after my so-called friends realized I was stronger than that, eventually they stopped asking me. If they wanted to throw their life away, by all means, that was their business; but I refused to hit rock bottom with them. I knew they would more than likely end up like my mother or worse.

To parents: Be a leader and show us how to become leaders. I respect parents who teach their children values. To all the teenagers out there, if you have a mother, father, or someone who provides for you the best that they can, you don't realize how blessed you are. For those who don't appreciate what their parents are doing for them, please put yourself in my shoes. Sometimes I wore my mother's shoes to school because I had none; I wore pants with holes in them because I had none. I would sometimes wear a sweater to school in the winter because my winter coat was too little; sometimes I didn't eat lunch because we didn't have food at home; and sometimes I would walk five miles to school because I didn't have bus fare. If you were fortunate because your parents provided for you the best they could, kiss them and tell them thanks because they saved you from pain and suffering.

Marshall
Age: 17

What was it like growing up? I was raised with both parents; my mother and father fought all the time. My brothers and sisters and I would try our best to help our mother, but that would make our father really angry; he would toss us like we were rag dolls. He didn't care if we were hurt or not. I can recall this particular time when he was beating my mother, my brother jumped in to defend my mother. My father picked up a huge piece of wood and started beating my brother. I wanted so badly to help, but I was terrified. We sat there and watched my brother lay in his blood; his body was badly bruised. We had a secret; my father told us whatever happened at home stayed at home.

What would you tell others to help them? Living with this secret was very painful, but I didn't tell anyone because I didn't want to be separated from my brothers and sisters; so we said nothing. As I grew into my teens with all the anger within me, I could have easily turned to crime as the solution, but I refused to be like my father. Instead, I used all my anger and every fiber of my body to improve in school; that was my way out. I realized the only way I could overcome this anger was to finish high school and go on to college.

Peer pressure: When there are things going on in your life, you don't have time for peer pressure. You are your best friend. So before you make any decisions, first take a moment and think it through. If you know it's wrong, don't do it, don't get caught up, and later pay a price for your criminal action, believe me it's not worth it.

To parents: You have to realize when you put your child in the middle of your battle, usually, trouble always follow them, or they follow trouble because they are accustomed to that lifestyle If you provide them with knowledge, more than likely they will make right decisions.

Lori
Age: 17

What was it like growing up? Both of my parents were alcoholics and drug addicts. My mother was doing drugs when I was born; my grandmother raised me from the age of two until she died when I was nine years old. After my grandmother died, I moved with my aunt; two years later, she died. My mother came to get me; it was hell from that time on. I remember on my thirteenth birthday, my stepfather made me drink; they said that was my birthday gift. I was so drunk that I got sick to my stomach; I didn't go to school for two days. Every holiday, they wanted me to drink with them; if I didn't, I could not celebrate the holiday.

What could you tell others to help them? No matter what you are going through, keep your head up, and remember, you are not by yourself. There are people in this world that are going through more than you could ever imagine.

Peer pressure: To all my peers who are dealing with family issues, the one thing you don't need is to surround yourself with trouble teenagers that will only make things worse. Everything I've been through in my life has been painful; the one thing that saved me from crime or getting in trouble with the law is my will to survive. The only way I could make that happen was to put everything I could into school. Yes, it was hard for me because I had parents who didn't care; my parents didn't want me to succeed in school. They did nothing to help me or provide for me. I started working in a small restaurant as a waitress. I had to make my own money as well as give my parents money; it was hard, but I did it, and you can too. Don't always look for the easy way out; challenge yourself to something a little difficult. I promise, it will make you a much stronger person. This is my last year in high school; finally, I can leave this behind to start a better life for me. I deserve that and so do you.

To parents: Parents are supposed to make life easier for us, not harder. I cannot understand, and I will never understand why a parent would cause their child to suffer, but I also believe what goes around comes around. You never know the damage you cause your child; hopefully they will survive like I did. Remember, one day you will need them, and you will, one day; and they just might not be there for you.

Gloria
Age: 16

What was it like growing up? Growing up was tough; we were evicted from every place we moved into. The longest we stayed in one place was probably six months. My mother would use the money for other things, especially her no-good, worthless boyfriend who didn't work because my mother would give him her welfare checks. She made sure he had the most expensive outfits even if she had to put it on hold. Her boyfriend dressed better than we did; he was her number one priority. I started working when I was fifteen years old to take care of me and my brother and sister. I remember when my mother made me buy her boyfriend a designer outfit for his birthday. She said he was the man in the house, and we should all support him and be grateful he was there. The only thing he did for us was take from us. He never bought one single thing with his money because he never had any money.

What would you tell others to help them? Remember, you can change things if you really want to stay in school, even when you feel you can't. Do not give up; before you know it, you will graduate and move on to better things in life. I could barely read until I went to my teacher for help; if you are having any problems, find a teacher you feel comfortable with, ask them to help you during or after school. Be honest and let your teacher know what is going on in your home.

Believe me, people do care; and they are willing to help if you give them a chance. Don't be ashamed of yourself; be proud of yourself because you just made the right choice. Whatever you do, don't turn to violence, and do not drop out of school; if you make that decision, your life will only get worse. Remember, you are not by yourself, I am walking down that same road.

Peer pressure: Peer pressure is just another word for problems, and we all have those; remember, you don't need friends. If they mean you no good, find a true friend, someone you can talk to, someone who wants what is right for you.

To parents: I see so many poor parents who are bad examples for their children; the sad thing, they think it's normal and that they are doing no wrong. If you really want to know the truth, ask your child what kind of parent are you. I just hope they tell you the truth even if it hurts. But I truly believe, you already know.

Vickie
Age: 17

What was it like growing up? I was raised by my mother and stepfather; he and my mother got married when I was four years old. My mother had two other children by my stepfather; he thought the world of my brother and sister. Sometimes he would take them on vacation in the summer to visit his family, but he never took me with him. For the first time when I turned fourteen, he took my brother, sister, and me out of town to a family reunion; my mother didn't go because she had just started her new job.

Some of my stepfather's relatives and I went swimming. I noticed him watching me; but to me, he was like my father since I had no other father. After swimming, my stepfather took me back to the hotel to change clothes; my brother and sister didn't go. While I was taking a shower, my stepfather came into the shower with me; he told me to never tell anyone especially my mother. I knew if I told my mother, she would be devastated; eventually, I had to tell because I got pregnant. My mother asked me, how many times did it happen? I told her once. she forgave him; she said everyone is entitled to one mistake. I wanted an abortion, but my stepfather said no. After I had my son, my stepfather told me that any decisions I make about my son had to be made by him because he was my child's father.

What would you tell others to help them? If you are living with a secret, remember that's your business; but sometimes talking about it with someone you can trust can be the best thing for you. We all make mistakes; no one is poppet, and no one has the right to judge you. But of course, people always do. More than likely; they also have skeletons in their closet. So don't be ashamed of something that is not your fault. To get over something that is bothering you, get involved with positive things. Once you do that, all your negative energy will slowly fade away. Keep your head up and your self-esteem high eventually; you will get through it sooner than you think, only if you don't let it get the best of you.

Pregnancy: Having a child was something I didn't plan. I always knew raising a child was expensive and hard work, something I was not ready for. Now that I have my son, as a parent, I have to work twice as hard to provide for my son and me. Of course, that means graduating from high school and completing college. I want the best for my child because he deserves that. The hard thing about raising a baby at my age is you have no freedom. I went from a teenager to a woman in nine months; if you think it's easy, believe me, it is not. Before you decide to have a baby, go to someone whom you know is an excellent parent, ask someone who will tell you the truth. If you don't know of anyone, all I can say is be ready to say good-bye to freedom and hello to motherhood, twenty-four hours, seven days a week.

Peer pressure: Some people can handle peer pressure, and others can't find someone who can give them good advice and use it.

To parents: Having a close relationship with your child will only make life better for you and your child.

Randy
Age: 17

What was it like growing up? My mother was a single mother of three; she provided for us the best she could. She made sure we had things we needed even if she had to work overtime. My mother was kind of strict; she was involved in school activities. She was at school meetings, parent conference meeting, she did her best.

She made sure we did our homework. She made sure we had food, shelter, and clothing; but most of all, she instilled values and mortals in us. My mother didn't date a lot, but the few men she did date were well respectable men. I am proud to say that my mother is a very intelligent and an attractive forty-six-year-old woman. On Sundays, we were in church singing and giving praises to God.

What would you tell others to help them? Sometimes we don't realize how blessed we really are, just because things seem hard, and you are going through something in your life; remember, trouble only last a little while. The only thing you should be thinking about is school. Make the best of it; you don't have to be an A+ student in order to achieve. If your grades are Cs and Ds and you are trying your best, keep trying, and your grades will improve even more. If you can't study at home, go to a library for one hour each day, or go to a friend's house and study together, and you will eventually see some improvements in your grades. You are worth more than you think; remember, every doctor and lawyer were not an A+ student. The difference between you and them is they believed in themselves, and they were not going to let anyone stop them from achieving their goals. Remember, whatever you wish to be is entirely up to you, not someone else.

Peer pressure: You control peer pressure; don't let peer pressure control you. If some told you to jump off the bridge, would you be stupid enough to actually do it? I hope not, because that is what peer pressure is, a simple yes or no. If you don't know how to speak up and tell someone where to get off, you better learn.

You control; don't be stupid and let someone control you. Learn how to say *no, no, no, no, no*; it's easy practice saying no if you don't know how. Once you say no and the person don't like it, if they walk away and never speak to you again, guess what, you won; move on to other friends, one who has the same goals as yourself.

To parents: Being a parent is one of the hardest tests there is. My mother's parenting skills taught me to become the best man I could ever be; my respect for young ladies is deep and beyond. My mother taught us morals and respect; the same values and respect she also have for herself will follow me everywhere I go. This is my last year in high school; my grade point average is 3.8. I will be attending the same college my siblings attend. I can truly say that my mother paved a way for us, and she made life easier and worth living. I hope I can find and marry a young lady like my mother.

Tina
Age: 17

What was it like growing up? Having sex, parting, and hanging out with my mother and her friends were quite normal; at least I thought it was until my mother was arrested for selling cocaine. This particular day, my mother, her friend and I went to a backyard party. I was fourteen, but everyone thought I was eighteen; my mother told me to let them think that and not to tell them anything different. My mom met some guy at the party; they started talking, my mother went to the car, and the next thing I saw was my mother getting handcuff. The police surrounded my mother's car; after searching her car, they found cocaine in the trunk of the car. I had no idea my mother had cocaine in her car; the police was told I was her daughter, and they then asked me my age. Because they were the police, I had no choice but to tell them the truth; once they found out I was fourteen, that gave them more of a reason to arrest my mother. The next thing I knew, I was in foster care; my mother is serving ten years in prison. Although I miss my mother, I do believe it was the best thing for me. My foster mother is more of a mother than my real mother could ever be. I'm in school every day; my grades improved from Ds to B. I realize how important education really is. I participate in after school activities; my life is now in order by the time my mother is released from prison. I will have my bachelor's degree in engineering. Hopefully, my mother has her life in order as well; if not, I will end my daughter-mother relationship with my mother.

What would you tell others to help them? I understand that sometimes things are forced upon us, especially if our parent or guardian is in control; sometimes we do things, and we have no control. Believe me, I truly understand; if that is the case, please go to someone for help, someone you can trust. Sometimes our involvement has a big impact on our lives, but you can also control what is happening in your life. The only way out of a good or bad situation is completing high school so you can go on to college, at least that's one thing no one can take away from you. Remember to put all your anger, frustration, and everything you have into school; when you do, you will come out on top. Remember, your life can get a lot better if you aim high, reach deep down inside you; we all have it, but it's up to us to believe we can do anything if we try.

Peer pressure: Sometimes our own family can be our peer pressure; remember one thing, another person's problems do not have to become your problem. You don't have to accept the things that are happening in your life; you don't have to like the things that are happening in your life just because you don't like your situation at the present time. Remember, you can change all of that if you believe in yourself, stay focused, and stay in school.

To parents: I hope my mother read my story as a parent; you are supposed to protect and set examples for your child. Parents are not and should not bring harm upon their child. My foster mother taught me value and respect; I never had that because of my foster mother. I am a stronger and confident person.

Kimberly
Age: 17

What was it like growing up? My father raised my brother and me. I never met my mother; she left my father when I was born. My brother at the time was two years old. It was told to us that my mother remarried and has another family. My father said my mother found her high school sweetheart, divorced my father, and moved to another state with her high school sweetheart. My father is disabled; he was injured in a bad car accident, which was when my mother left him, actually two weeks after his accident. During the time when my father was in rehab, my father's mother took care of my brother and me. My father started caring for my brother and me when I was six months old. My father is in a wheelchair; he is paralyzed from the waist down. My father took care of my brother and me the best he could. He never missed a school function; he always had people to bring him. Somehow he would find a way. I remember this one time, my father didn't receive his SSI check; someone stole it. We had no food; my father's only concern was my brother and I having nothing to eat. Every morning, my father would leave the house to find work anywhere because he wanted us to have. My father came home with enough money to buy us grocery; my father ate canned soup for a month, but he cooked hot meals for my brother and me. Because my father is in a wheelchair, people tend to take advantage of him. My father has been robbed numerous times and was beaten. My father is my hero, my best friend. When I turned fourteen, I started hanging out with the wrong crowd of people. Everything they did was wrong; they had no respect for anyone. One day, I got into an argument with this guy whom I thought was my homeboy; the argument was not that serious.

My father told me time and time again to stop hanging with the crowd I was hanging around. I thought everything was okay, and my father didn't like them because they were my friends; to me, they were okay. The same week, this guy and I got into an argument. I was in school; my father was at home. The guy and his cousin broke into the house and badly beat and stabbed my father, almost ending his life. They told my father he had a choice, either he could get beaten or stabbed, or I could; my father told them to hurt him and not me. They did just that. My father was hospitalized for three weeks because he was stabbed in his lungs; he is now on oxygen. He cannot breathe on his own for a long amount of time. I blame myself for being stupid; if I had listened to my father in the beginning, this would not have happened. I couldn't ask for a better father; my father is my hero and my best friend. I no longer hang around with people who are bad influence and want nothing out of life. My friends now are truly a blessing. They help me care for my father. My brother is away at college. I will also be attending college in the fall; my grandmother will be caring for my father since he no longer can care for himself. The guys who attacked my father were sentenced to twenty-five years in prison.

What would you tell others? Every time I look at my father, I blame myself; there is no way around it. I try so hard to not blame myself; but the more I try, the worse I feel. When we make bad decisions, we know what we are doing. I knew the people I was hanging around were not good people. I knew it, I felt it. At that time, I didn't care because I was mad. I was mainly mad because I didn't have a mother to love me, and I wanted that so bad; so instead, I turned to violence as the answer. My father knew from the beginning, and he tried to tell me. I will never forgive myself for the pain I cause my innocent father when all he tried to do was protect me.

Peer pressure: Peer pressure affects everyone differently; some people are strong minded and can handle anything in a respectable manner. The one thing I would like to say is, no matter how angry and bitter you may feel because you don't like the way things are in your life, just hold on to that little thing called hope. As teenagers, we sometimes think we know it all; we don't care about who we are hurting. All we want to do is have fun, hang out with our friends, sneak to have sex, get high, drink alcohol, skip school, meet different people of the opposite sex, drop out of school, party, and some of us wanna get pregnant because we think we are in love, and think we are going to spent the rest of our lives with that person (*wrong*). For the last year, I have been to high schools talking to teenagers about all the things I mentioned above. There are so many teenagers that are lost, but I can truly say majority of the teenagers I talked to are smart, and they want something out of life. There are more teenagers that have HIV than any group of people, why? Because we don't take sex seriously, because we don't understand.

The only thing we know is we just like it, and we like being with different partners, which is why so many teenagers have HIV. Let me ask you this and be honest. If you meet someone and you really liked that person and you had a chance to go to bed with that person but you were HIV positive, would you tell that person? Now remember, once you tell that person, the chances are that person would say *no*; and from that moment on, more people will know you have HIV. Listen, I'm not stupid. I already know what the answer would be, that is why so many teenagers have HIV because no one is telling the other person; the only thing they are thinking about at the moment is *sex*. *Let's get it on* because my hormones are kicking. Guess what? you probably just came in contact with HIV because you were being *stupid* because you wanted *sex* right then, right now. Fifteen minutes of pleasure may now cause you your life; the bottom line is it's not worth it. Listen, you can beat the odds. First of all, you should say *no* to sex, but I know so many of us will not do that. At least, protect yourself with protection; but more than anything, graduate from high school and go on to college. Respect your body and yourself; and remember, you are not by yourself. We all have problems. Oh, did I forget to tell you I'm HIV positive? The question is who gave it to me? I will probably never know. I am seventeen. I started having sex when I was fourteen. I had four partners, and I know the names of them all, but the sad thing is no one is talking. None of them will take a test to find out.

To parents: First, I would like to tell my father I'm sorry for all the pain and sorrow I caused him. To parents, talk to your child about sex; my father told me about sex when I was twelve years old. The only problem is I wasn't listening. I forgot everything he told me during that passionate moment. So again, keep talking to them until you are blue in the face and protect them with protection if you know what I mean.

Felicia
Age: 16

What was it like growing up? I grew up without knowing who my parents were. I was six months when I went into foster care. I was told my mother was abusive to my sisters and brothers and me as well. I had broken ribs and a broken leg when I was removed from my parent's home. My sister and brothers were adopted by some other family. I have no idea where they are. My foster mother, who is now my adoptive mother, has always told me the truth about my biological mother whom I wish never to meet. The little I know about her is very painful. I often wonder how could she have a peaceful sleep at night, how could she live with herself and have peace within herself? I can recall the times when my mother would say to me, "I know I didn't have you from my belly, but I know I had you from my heart." I felt proud and loved from the very beginning. Of course, I wondered from time to time what my mother looked like. Did she think about me? I guess you can say I was confused; and yes, at times I feel like a peace of the puzzle was missing, but I'm not sure if I want to find it.

What would you tell others to help them? If you are someone who is adopted or in a foster home, remember one thing: God doesn't make mistakes. Our life was written before we entered into this world; and if God said this is how it is going to be in the beginning, then this is how it is. But God also said we all are created equal, which means whatever we want out of life, we can get it; the only different is some may have to work a little harder than others. Just because you weren't born with a silver spoon in your mouth does not make you any less of a person; actually, I think it's good to work a little harder because it makes you a stronger and better person. So when you feel you can't go on and you hate everyone and everything, just remember one thing: God is the only one who can fix it. Just call on him, and he will make it right; just believe in him, and pray to him every day morning, noon, and night and watch as he begins to make your life better. Find peace in your heart, and learn to forgive others; remember, the road you are walking, and the pain you are feeling will only make you a better a person because I have walked that same road, and I definitely felt the pain.

Peer pressure: We think because we are teenagers that we have a long life ahead of us when actually we don't. There are so many teenagers that are being killed or badly injured because of stupid decisions they make; that's why it is very important to surround yourself with positive, motivating teenagers. If you feel that's not important, you better think again; just look around you.

Brian
Age: 17

What was it like growing up? My parents were married for twenty-eight years; we were not rich. Both of my parents were everyday working parents; although we were not rich, we always felt like we were because that was how our parents made us feel. My parents had a beautiful relationship. Every night before they would go to bed, I could hear them talking about life, their jobs, relationships, and of course us; everything was positive. Yes, at times, they would fuss, but they never disrespected one another by using bad language. My parents were the everyday American parents. Every Sunday, you better believe, we were in church singing the good old gossip. I can remember just like any another kid not wanting to go to church, but of course, it wasn't happening; my parents made me. Both of my parents came from unstable households. My mother's parents were alcoholics and abusive; my father's mother was a drug addict. He never met his father; he was in and out of foster homes. If my parents would have never told me, I wouldn't believe it, because they raised us with values. My parents said everything they went through in life made them a better person and stronger person. It only proves that no matter what you go through as a child, it is up to you to make something of your own life.

What would you tell others to help them? Everybody live different lives; even if you come from the same household, your life will be different from your siblings. One will stay on the right path, and the other one might not.

You have to remember, life is a way you make it to be. When someone say they don't like life, to me, that means they don't like living. When you don't like living, you lose all respect for yourself and others. Remember, life did nothing to you, so don't blame the world, or be angry at the world because things are not going your way. When things in your life seem hard and you get angry and frustrated, remember, it's okay to feel that way because there is not one person in this world who never had problems or trouble. But it is your decision on how to fix it and make it better. Either you stay on the right path, or have the I-don't-care-about-anything attitude. Once you begin to feel like that, guess what? More problems and trouble will come right to you.

Peer pressure: Peer pressure to me is just an excuse teenagers use. I'm sure half the people really don't know what it means. I did it because my friends did it, or they told me to do it; don't be stupid. If you know someone is getting ready to do something wrong, why in the hell would you let him convince you to commit a crime with him. Check this out homeboy and homegirl. They might talk a good game, but they don't have your back. As soon as you turn your back, I promise you, they will stab you in it.

To parents: The sad thing about some parents, especially the ones who set no guidelines, morals, and values, is that they really think they are good parents; they don't know wrong from right. Listen, if you really want to know the truth about your parenting skills, just ask your kids or someone who you know, will tell you the truth. Remember, the truth always hurt.

Fran
Age: 17

What was it like growing up? My grandparents raised me; ever since I was three years old, my mother was diagnosis as bipolar. She was on every medication you could think of. The times I did spent with her were very painful because she would do things and not know why she did it. This one time, she was cooking; and for no reason, she took the food and threw it across the room. She said the food burned her hand so she got mad at the food. Another time, she and I were talking, at least we tried to talk; she asked me a question, we started laughing, and, all of sudden, she got mad at me and told me not to talk to her anymore. I can actually write a book on my mother's behavior. I truly believe that with all the medications she was taking caused her condition to be worse.

What would you tell others to help them? No matter what you are going through in life, good or bad, there is someone going through the same thing or worse.

Peer pressure: Don't think you need friends in order to fit in with the crowd. If you feel you knew a friends, find someone with the same characteristics as yours.

To parents: I don't blame God or my mother for her problem. I accept my mother for who she is. I will be attending college this year, and I hope, one day, I will be able help her financially, emotionally, and spiritually.

Lizzie
Age: 17

What was it like growing up? My aunt Diana raised me; she is and has always been more of a mother than my own mother. My mother lived with every man that took her in; she never had her own place; and she was never stable. My aunt refused to let my mother stay with her because of the kind of person she is; my mother would steal from anyone to support her drugs and alcohol. She lost custody of my other sisters and brothers who are in foster home. I believe the two younger ones are adopted. My aunt has always treated me like a daughter. I never felt any difference from her other children. My mother is jealous of the relationship I have with my aunt. I know when the day comes for me to get married, I want my aunt to be in the front roll. The only time I do see my mother is the few times when she comes to see me. I can't visit her because she doesn't have her own home.

What would you tell others to help them? We never know what other people are going through; the kids at my high school think my aunt is my mother. I haven't told them anything different because it's really not their business. It's not that I'm ashamed of my mother. I just don't like talking about it because it hurts; although I appreciate and love my aunt dearly for everything she has done for me, it still saddens me not to have my mother in my life. I know I'm not the only person who is and have experiences of not having a parent in their life. So to all my friends who know what I'm talking about, we are in this together. And we will get through this together.

Peer pressure: Not having my mother in my life is enough peer pressure for me. I can't afford mentally and physically to deal with any other pressure.

To parents: I believe parents who chose drugs or alcohol instead of raising their children are selfish because the way they chose to live their life is their decision. If a person really and truly wants to stop using drugs, they can because if they can't, why can some people stop? They stop because they want to. I don't care if you have to struggle to stop your child; it's worth struggling for.

Marvin
Age: 16

What was growing up like? Growing up to me was not the best. My mother struggled and worked hard; she cleaned houses for a living; and she dropped out of school at an early age. She didn't have a trade or college degree; she took care of us the best she could with the little she had. I love my mother with all my heart; she would go without just so we could have, that to me is a true mother. Our father removed himself from our lives and moved to another state with his wife and other children. He didn't support my mother in any way; he never came to see us or even called us on the phone. It's definitely not because he couldn't find us because we've been in the same house for over twenty years. I remember my mother catching the bus to go and clean houses. Everywhere she went, she would catch a bus proudly; and she never missed any of our ceremonies at school. I have two brothers and two sisters; we all made a deal to graduate from college so we could support our mother, so she would never have to work again in her life.

What would you tell others? Make the best of your life and never forget the ones who took care of you, especially your parents.

Peer pressure: Never rush into anything; take your time and think before you do it.

To parents: If you take care of your children and be a parent to those children, they will in return be there for you. Remember, one day you will need them to help you; that is why it is important for parents to teach their children to have values and mortals.

Candace
Age: 17

What was it like growing up? My brother and I lived with our father and his wife, the witch; she was very ungrateful. My father treated her as if she was some Cinderella, what a fairy tale or, should I say, scary tale. She looked like she belonged on broom; the only thing that was missing was the motor to the broom. She didn't work; my father supported the whole family, even her three kids. My father worked three jobs so he could support everybody. My brother and I are very close because all we have is each other. My mother lived with her lesbian lover; when my father found out, he came and got us. He was very uncomfortable with the situation; my brother was also against my mother's relationship. My father's wife would take trips, at least three times out of the year, using my dad's money for her luxury. There have been times when I wanted to introduce my dad to my friend's mom because she was single, ambitious, and pretty. Knowing the kind of man my dad is, he wouldn't accept the offer.

Hopefully one day, soon my dad will wake up and realize he no longer wants to be married to the wicked witch of the east.

What can you tell others to help them? Sometimes we may not approve of our parent's mate, when actually it's not our business. I believe the only time it is our business or our concern will be if it's an abusive relationship. Although I don't care for my father's wife, I still have respect for her because if my father is happy with the relationship, then I have no choice but to accept it.

Peer pressure: I don't get involved with stupid stuff. I have one best friend, and I don't want anymore. When you have a lot of friends, trouble is around the corner; although sometimes a person doesn't have to know you in order to like you. If a person doesn't like you and you never did anything to them, whatever you do, don't kiss their a—just to be their friend. Actually, you should be glad to not have a friend like that; a person who feels like that usually has low self-esteem about themselves, so don't get caught up in the bull crap. You are much too better for that.

To parents: I often wonder what went wrong with a lot of the parents today. There are few role models for today's generation. There are more parents using drugs, more grandparents are raising their grandchildren, more fathers are walking away from their responsibility, and more relationships are ending in divorces. If we don't have our parents for role models, then whom do we have?

Mike
Age: 17

What was it like growing up? I was raised by my mother and stepfather; my stepfather is more than a father than my real father. As a matter of fact, he is the only father I know; he supported me in everything I did, especially sport. He was the little league coach; he participated in everything my siblings and I joined. My father worked a full-time and part-time job; he supported the family 100 percent. My mother worked and supported only herself; every week, she had new outfit. She hung out with her friends; sometimes she stayed out all night. She was wild, dude, I mean wild; she was fifteen years younger than my father. I believe the only reason why she was with him was because he was a good provider. She didn't care about him, and he knew it; he always said when we got older, he was going to leave because she didn't appreciate him. I couldn't blame him at all for leaving; I know I would have done the exact same thing.

Peer pressure: I'm too ambitious to hang out with people who have no purpose in life; my plans are to graduate and go to college so I can play pro baseball. The best years of your life are the prime times, why waste it on stupid stuff? The best time to be accepted in anything is when you're in your teens to early twenties; there is no way in hell I'm going to miss out on the opportunity.

To parents: Will the real parents please stand up?

Lindsay
Age: 17

What was it like growing up? My aunt and uncle adopted me when I was a baby; actually, they brought me home from the hospital. Both of my parents were addicted to drugs when I was born; I had drugs in my system; my parents told me I would have very bad withdraws; and I cried constantly. I thank God for my aunt and uncle because they never gave up on me; they could very easily gave me up for adoption, but they didn't. At times, I have a hard time comprehending in school. I have to work a little harder than others. This is my last year in high school, I will be attending college to further my education. School helps me in many ways; I don't look at it as being boring because you have to sit in class all day. Actually, it's the one place that prepares you for bigger and better things. You have to have your education in order to go on to bigger and better things in life. The bottom line, school helps build your self-esteem because it makes you feel good as a person; if it doesn't, you are looking at it for all the wrong reasons. Stay focused, and before you know it, you will be graduating, and the next step is college. And before you know it, you will be graduating from college as well, entering in the wonderful world of business and success. At least that's one thing no one can take away from you is your education. At times, I wanted to give up on school because for me it was really hard. Once I sincerely thought about it, I realized my life will only become much more harder and difficult if I give up on my education. After seriously thinking about it and being honest about it, I begin to look at school in a positive way. Once you make a decision and you know it's the right one, you feel good about yourself.

That is why it is so important not to let anyone stop you from achieving your goals, your destiny. Let's be real; when you are with negative people, you begin to think and feel like negative people. You can't see your future because to you it doesn't exist; the only thing you see is staying in trouble or getting in trouble. You can't be negative and positive at the same time; so either you go forward in life or backward, it's your decision. People who are successful and happy with life are the ones who choose to go forward in life. The people who stay in and out of trouble, get involved with drugs, they don't want anything out of life because they think little of themselves and choose to go backward in life. So don't be mad or jealous at other people because they choose to go forward in life. Remember, the decision is yours.

What would you tell others to help them? By all means, I am not saying I'm perfect because no one is perfect, but we can correct our problems. Stop getting mad at people who are telling you the truth about yourself when you know you are wrong. Have you ever thought for one moment that these people are only trying to help you and save you from trouble? Everybody is not against you, for what reason would he be against you? Just because they don't like your attitude does not mean they don't like you as a person. So stop being so angry and listen. Remember, no one owes you anything, not even your parents. Sometimes when we become teenagers, we think we know everything because we experience sex because we are in love; at least that's what we think or because we are being with someone older. Believe me, that does not make you older because of the negative things you experienced.

Peer pressure: Don't let people convince you to do things you know in your heart is wrong. I believe we all have a good person who lives inside of us, and it's up to us to find that person. Anyone can do wrong or live wrong or even make wrong decisions; as a matter of fact, those kinds of people are inviting the devil into their heart because as we all know the devil mean us no good, and he doesn't want us to have good within our heart. He wants us to think devilish and be angry with everyone, hurt and kill people. He wants us not to like our parents and siblings for whatever reason. He wants us to not like people; he wants us to have attitudes with others. He wants us to talk about people, even if we don't really know the person. He wants us to be jealous of others; he wants us to rob and steal from people. He wants us not to have respect for others and ourselves. He wants us to befriend others. He wants us to hurt our parents and not respect our parents; he does not care if they gave us life. He wants you to do drugs and have sex because he doesn't want you to respect your body, and he doesn't care if you catch some disease. He wants you to be a criminal; he wants you to be in and out of trouble with the law. He wants you to be the worse human being you could possibly be; he doesn't care if you're an infant or an older person. He wants *you*. He enjoys controlling your thinking, your mind, body, and spirit as long as you are acting like this; guess what? He loves it. He got you just where he wants you; the sad thing you probably don't realize it because you think it's you. He enjoys fooling you; he doesn't want you to realize the good in you. That's why he has to keep you busy thinking wrong and doing wrong from the time you wake up until the time you go to bed.

The only way you can get him off your back is *pray, pray,* and *pray*; ask God to help you change so you can be a better person. Take it one day at a time; start doing things that are right; and start thinking positive. Find peers who are positive and mean well. Stop doing things that will cause you trouble and pain. Start believing in yourself; make a change in your life for the better, and eventually, doors will open for you. You can have whatever you want in life if you start doing what is right in life; it's that easy. Once you beginning praying to God, asking him to help you change, you will become a better person; remember, God knows you better than you know yourself; and you cannot fool God. If you really want to change, he will come into your heart and help change you to become a better person.

Mark
Age: 18

What was it like growing up? I grow up in the city project with eight brothers and sisters. We were dirt poor; my mother was on drugs ever since I could remember.

We all had different fathers; my father was in prison for murder. I can count the times on one hand I ever seen him; each time I visited him was very painful. This was my true blood father; when I look at him, I see me from head to toe, the way he walks, the way he talks, and everything. To me, he was calm, cool, and smooth. I never once asked him about the incident that took place fifteen years ago because I didn't know how and in a way I was afraid to hear the truth; everyone tells me it was self-defense. When my friends would ask me about my father, I could never tell them the truth.

I always felt if people founded out, they would treat me differently; although most of my friends didn't have their fathers in their lives either, they were not in prison for murder. The sad thing is I never had any respect for Deanna, my mother. We were evicted from every apartment we moved to. We never lived in a house with a backyard or front porch. We lived in a two-bedroom apartment with eight children. Four of my siblings are in foster homes. I have no idea where they are actually. I haven't seen them in over five years. Two of my older siblings are in college after being adopted by a family. My brother and I are twins; we share an apartment together. We also attend college, studying biology. After living the life we lived, I decided when I was in my early teens I wanted a better life for myself. Being poor was something I wanted to put behind me because it was too painful. I remember many nights we would go to bed hungry because we had nothing to eat; we would mix sugar and water together because it was all we had. My mother was in the streets getting high. I'm talking spaced-out high. I remember walking to school, I would see her in the alley searching for food or bottles. I would keep walking, hoping she didn't know who I was. My brother and I called the authorities on my mother so they would take my siblings and place them in foster home. After we made the call, we hid so they wouldn't find us; we saw as they placed our little sisters and brothers in the car and drove away. I was happy because I knew my little sisters and brothers were going to be safe, and I was sad because I knew I would probably never see them again.

My brother and I stayed with whomever we could because we didn't want to go into a foster home; we knew more than likely they were going to separate us. At age fifteen, we did what we had to do in order to survive: we worked at fast food restaurants; we cleaned floors; we worked in gas stations; we delivered newspaper; and we worked just about any job in order to survive. Although we didn't graduate from high school, we did get our GED. We enrolled in college; ever since then, our life has changed for the better.

What would you tell others to help them? Always know this: there is nothing you can't do if you put your mind to it. I don't care if you grew up poor and your parents were abusive or drug addicts or if they were not in your life for whatever reason. If you grew up in and out of foster homes, if you were rich, if your parents were the CEO of some large company, or if they were successful business owners remember, your life is your life, not your mother's, father's, sister's, or brother's; it belongs to you. The way I grew up, I could have very easily turned to crime as the answer because I didn't care about anything. I didn't know anything about respect or how to be kind to others because I was not taught those things. I didn't know right from wrong or should I say I didn't care; school was not important to me. I didn't know anything about being successful because I was not taught those things. I didn't know I could drive a Porsche or have all the money I wanted without selling drugs because I was not taught those things. I didn't know if I robbed or stole from somebody, it was a crime because I was not taught those things. I didn't know doing drugs would eventually destroy the body and mind because I was not taught those things. I didn't know hanging out with friends who were trouble would cause me trouble because I was not taught those things. I didn't know if I shot and killed someone, I was wrong because I didn't have a conscience. I wasn't taught morals and values.

I had to learn these things on my own because I didn't have parents or relatives to tell me the important facts of life. I had to stop being jealous of what others had and realize they worked for what they had. I had to tell myself I could have it as well. Everything I knew was negative. I had to teach myself to become positive. I began praying, asking God to help me because I couldn't understand me as a person. Each day I began to do little things that were positive. I began to remove myself slowly from troubled people. I began to stop listening to people who talked negative about others. I began to surround myself with positive people like my peers. I began to stop thinking negative and started thinking positive about life and people. I started telling myself every day I wanted a better life. I wanted something good in life. I don't care how hard I have to work. I was willing to work to get it. Every time I started thinking negative, I would stop myself and begin thinking about positive things; eventually, I trained my mind to start believing in myself. Remember whatever situation you are in at the moment, there is a way out as long as you are still breathing; it is not over for you, and because of that, this is your chance to turn your life around for you and only you. Don't worry about your family or friends if people can't understand; you want something better in life. Remove them from your life. If you don't, your blessing will never come. Remember, God can't bless you if you surround yourself with negative, troubled people. God can't bless you if you keep getting in trouble. God can't bless you if you keep doing wrong. Just try it; believe me, you can do it. Stop thinking you can't; sometimes we think so little of ourselves that we sometimes don't realize our brain can take on more than we think. Finish high school or get your GED, enroll in college or take up a trade, do something with your life, and the day you do, you will begin to feel like a winner.

Starting today, let's start respecting others and ourselves, especially our parent's and our elderly; remember, everybody is not against you, especially if they don't know you. When you start changing and looking at life in a positive way, it is up to you to not let people turn you back around; keep going forward, and eventually doors will open for you.

From the Author

I truly hope after reading about these teenagers, you have a change of attitude or you will continue to stay focused. Whatever the case may be, you are responsible for your actions. No one can make you do anything you do not wish to do, which is why I firmly believe it is extremely important whom you surround yourself with. Whom you select as a friend or mate will have a strong impact on you as an individual. If you are someone who wants something out of life and is working toward those goals, you cannot surround yourself with negative peers who do not want the same thing. Majority of the time, when that happens, eventually it will detract you from succeeding. Remember, you cannot change a person who is not ready to change; and if they are trying to change for all the right reasons, believe me, they do not need your help in order to do so. I see so many young teenagers who are smart and intelligent but for some reason make wrong decisions; some get involved in unhealthy relationships, and others select the wrong people as friends.

You may be smart and intelligent in some ways, but you are *dumb* when it comes to common sense. I'm sure if you have parents or someone who cares about your well-being, they tried telling you over and over again about the wrong decision you are making. Some teenagers feel they have to do whatever it takes just to fit in with the wrong crowd. Some start drinking alcohol, some start doing every kind of drugs you can think of, some start experiencing sex not realizing the danger behind it, and some turn to criminal behavior. I realize I am not your mother or father, and I don't know you, but I am someone who cares about your future.

I worked in the juvenile facility, and yes, I've seen it all more than I ever imagined. The teenagers you read about in this book were willing to reach out to help you so you won't make the same mistakes half of them made, but it is entirely up to you to take their advice. Stay focused or get focused before it's too late; remember, it's easy to get in trouble, but it is hard to get out of trouble. Once you enter into the juvenile system, your life and your decisions are no longer yours. I don't care how you grew up, wealthy or poor, with drug addict parents or parents who were successful and very much involved in your life; remember your life belongs to you, so don't let anyone or anything cause you to destroy your life. You don't need anyone to tell you, you are somebody because deep down inside, you know you are.

My Dear Parents

Being a mother of a fifteen-year-old daughter, I am beginning to see a change in my daughter's attitude and personality. I noticed when she was twelve years old and younger, she listened more and did exactly what I asked of her with no ifs, buts, and maybes. The day my daughter turned thirteen, I witnessed a change; it was almost an overnight change in her attitude. My little girl, my baby, is now a teenager. It is so amazing how our bodies go through changes from a young child into adolescent, from adolescent into adulthood, from adulthood through menopause, at least with women; and with every hormonal change that our body experiences, the mind is affected the most. The day my daughter turned thirteen, I remember it as if it was yesterday; it was an early Friday morning.

I kissed her and said happy birthday, gave her a birthday card with money in the envelope, and I told her the day was her day, and what exactly did she want to do? I thought everything was okay because she was happy; a half hour later, I went downstairs to check on her. She was crying for no apparent reason at all. When I asked her what was wrong, she said nothing. I asked her again why she was crying; her response was she didn't know why. She was crying really hard. She is my only child so I never experienced this before as a concerned mother. I began asking her questions; some questions, I must admit, were little extreme. I almost started crying myself. I began asking her, "Did someone upset you? Is someone mad with you? Did someone hurt you? Was it something I did or said?" I even asked my daughter with fear in my heart and tears in my eyes, "You're not having sex, are you?" She looked at me and shouted, "NO, MOM!" Although I know my daughter is not sexually active at that moment, I didn't know what to think; after I asked my daughter that, I really felt stupid. Until this day, I have no idea why my daughter was crying. I believe she also has no idea herself. I truly believe that particular day my daughter's hormones were kicking. That is why it is so important for us as parents to have some kind of connection with our children as they go through their changes, especially during their adolescent years.

Don't wait until your children are teenagers before you begin a relationship with your child; the moment your child enters into this world should be the day you bond with your child until the day you depart from this world. As parents, it is our job to teach our children values and morals so as they grow from adolescent to adulthood they will have respect for themselves and others. After working in the juvenile facilities, I clearly understand why teenagers are in juvenile detention; these teenagers are not taught how to respect or love themselves. They have very low self-esteem. It is not their fault because they feel this way; parents who have no respect and have low self-esteem for themselves cannot be a role model for their children. It is impossible. You have parents who sell drugs and use drugs, parents who have children from every man and woman they lay down with, parents who use profanity at their children every time they up their mouth, parents who drink alcohol like it's water, parents who party every week instead of spending quality time with their children. You have deadbeat fathers and mothers who remove themselves from parenthood as if it's an option; you have parents who treat their children like a best friend instead of being a parent. You have parents who talk negative to their children instead of encouraging them. You have parents who involve their children into their negative lifestyle like it's something to be proud of. You have parents who allow their children to do anything they want, even though they know it's wrong because they refuse to stand up and be a parent. You have parents who receive checks from the welfare system because they refuse to be independent and stand on their own two feet. You have parents who allow their children to talk to them any way they want because they decided to not stop them from the beginning.

You have parents who abuse their children as if they were some deranged person out in the street. You have parents who put themselves before their children because they are too selfish to attend to their children's needs first. You have parents who put other people first, like their mate, because they forgot about their responsibilities, and you have parents who *never* introduced their child to *Christ*, the number one problem solver.

Majorities of the teenagers that are in juvenile have experienced these problems. We as parents make parenting harder than what it is; no, I am not saying it's easy, but we can contribute to the problem as well. Being a parent is not just giving birth to a child and letting your child go astray. As mothers and fathers, we have to share in the responsibility if we want our children to grow and become productive citizens. As parents, we have to get along with one another because we are the ones who brought this child into this world. It is our responsibility to introduce our child to the positive things in life but most of all talk to our child about life. Develop a one-on-one relationship with your child;

tell your child how much you love them. Get involved in their school activities even if you don't want to. Do it for your child; no, I am not saying as parents we are not entitled to our own life. All I am saying is include them in your life; don't be selfish and forget about your child. Sometimes we get in a relationship, and we forget about our children. Sometimes we allow our mate or spouse dictate to us about our relationship with our children. Remember that is your child, your seed; a part of you lives within that child, and that is something that can never change. I am not speaking about all relationships because sometimes our spouse means well, and they speak the truth; and in some cases, they want their spouse to have a relationship with their child.

It is not always the other person's fault for why the parent is not in the child's life. That is why it is so important for the biological parents to have a friendly relationship for the child's sake only. As a single parent, I know I am doing an excellent job in raising my child. I make sure I don't put anyone before her. I let her know she is beautiful. I tell her whatever she wants out of life, she can receive it if she is willing to work for it. I spent quality time with her. I let her express herself to me, good or bad. I talk to her about life, and she knows about the Lord Jesus Christ. I tell her how much I love her. I teach her to respect herself and others, and I teach her morals and values. No, I am not saying my daughter is any better than any other child; but what I am saying is as her mother, I did the best I could with no regrets. If we teach our children love, respect, values, and morals, I truly believe our children will spread their wings and fly like an eagle.

I Know

I know who I am.
I know who I am, can no one stop me or stand in my way.
I know who I am, I don't care how people down-rate me.
I know who I am, I have total control over my life.
I know who I am, I don't need people to tell me.
I know who I am, I'm a leader not a damn follower.
I know who I am, can no one influence me to do wrong.
I know who I am, my friends wish they were me.
I know who I am, I'm creative and smart.
I know who I am, although my parents never told me.
I know who I am, I can do all things because my savior strengthens me.
I know who I am. The question is, do you know who you are?

Poem by Angel Flew

I Thought

I thought I would never become somebody because of how I grew up.

I thought I would never become somebody because of all the abuses I suffered as a child.

I thought I would never become somebody because of all the drugs my mother used when she was pregnant with me.

I thought I would never become somebody because my father was an ex-convict.

I thought I would never become somebody because people told me I would never be.

I thought I would never become somebody because I didn't believe in me.

I thought I would never become somebody because of all the wrong I did.

I though I would never become somebody because of my troubled past.

I thought I would never become somebody because I believed I couldn't

I thought I would never become somebody because no one believed in me.

I thought I would never become somebody until the day I started believing in me.

Poem by Angel Flew